W9-BVU-987

nothing is impossible

nothing is impossible

Women of Faith

THOMAS NELSON
Since 1798

NASHVILLE   DALLAS   MEXICO CITY   RIO DE JANEIRO

Published in Nashville, Tennessee, by Thomas Nelson. Thomas Nelson is a registered trademark of Thomas Nelson, Inc.

Thomas Nelson, Inc. titles may be purchased in bulk for educational, business, fund-raising, or sales promotional use. For information, please e-mail SpecialMarkets@ ThomasNelson.com.

Scripture quotations are taken from the following sources: The King James Version of the Bible (KJV). *The Message* (MSG) by Eugene H. Peterson. © 1993, 1994, 1995, 1996, 2000. Used by permission of NavPress Publishing Group. All rights reserved. The NEW AMERICAN STANDARD BIBLE® (NASB), © The Lockman Foundation 1960, 1962, 1963, 1968, 1971, 1972, 1973, 1975, 1977, 1995. Used by permission. The New Century Version® (NCV). © 2005 by Thomas Nelson, Inc. Used by permission. All rights reserved. The HOLY BIBLE: NEW INTERNATIONAL VERSION® (NIV). © 1973, 1978, 1984 by International Bible Society. Used by permission of Zondervan Publishing House. All rights reserved. THE NEW KING JAMES VERSION (NKJV). © 1982 by Thomas Nelson, Inc. Used by permission. All rights reserved. The *Holy Bible*, New Living Translation (NLT). © 1996, 2004. Used by permission of Tyndale House Publishers, Inc., Carol Stream, Illinois 60189. All rights reserved. The NEW REVISED STANDARD VERSION of the Bible (NRSV). © 1989 by the Division of Christian Education of the National Council of the Churches of Christ in the U.S.A. All rights reserved. *The Living Bible* (TLB). © 1971. Used by permission of Tyndale House Publishers, Inc., Wheaton, Illinois 60189. All rights reserved.

ISBN: 978-1-4002-0242-3

Printed in the United States of America

10 11 12 13 14 WC 6 5 4 3

Contents

Part 1

Nothing Is Impossible

MARY GRAHAM

She was absolutely beautiful. Long, shiny, jet-black hair pulled back from her face; brown eyes as rich and dark as liquid chocolate. She wore a caramel-colored jumpsuit. She was thirteen. I might have been sitting across from any of the thousands of teenage girls I've met at our Revolve Tour events in America, but I wasn't even close. Though Jenna Lucado from our Revolve Tour Team and this beautiful African teenager were sitting next to me, I couldn't have been farther from the Revolve Tour. I was in Ethiopia.

The teenager's name was Tsehay (pronounced "sigh"), and she lived with her grandmother, clearly the matriarch of their family, and her mother, who seemed quiet and shy. Several other family members were there, but it was hard to know who was related and who might have been visiting for the day. Clearly several families shared the small plot of ground, surrounded by a bamboo fence that contained several mud huts with thatched roofs. I could tell by looking they were one of the poorest households in her area.

We sat in the hot sun, listening intently as the director of the World Vision project in that village told us the heartbreaking story of what happened to Tsehay. As a World Vision-sponsored child, she was able to attend school, which clearly was the most important thing in her life. One day, slightly before dawn, while on the hour-long walk to school with other World Vision children, she was abducted by a young man and three of his friends. She fought to get away, but could not. Obviously, the men who took her recognized her as a child who had no strong defender or protector in her home. She tried to fight and escape, but clearly she could not protect herself. She screamed and cried, but no one could hear her among the trees and gorges.

The abductors ran with her to a nearby town. On the way, two men with guns stopped them. The men demanded the abductors release Tsehay to them, but her abductors would not. In fact, they said to the men with guns, "She is our sister. We are not abducting her." The gunmen offered to pay thirty dollars for her. That's when Tsehay boldly tried to protect herself. She said, "I am *not* their sister. They are abducting me."

It wasn't clear what happened in that transaction but, in the end, the abductors left with Tsehay. She lost her shoes on the twenty-four-mile, very rough and stony eight-hour walk. They took her to a small shack in town, raped her that very night and locked her in the room alone. For forty-five days, those who stole her set out to destroy her will and any personal power or sense of integrity she had. They believed that if they could "break" her, they could keep her subservient to their power and will. She was raped every day, sometimes more than once and by more than one man. Many days she never even saw sunlight.

As I heard the story, I felt the truth was too much to bear. It was so burdensome to even imagine what had happened to this beautiful young woman. But here she was, the picture of quiet peace. She seemed radiant and almost perfection as she sat before us. There had been other children with her on the road, and when Tsehay was kidnapped, they had run back to tell her grandmother what happened. The grandmother walked straight to the World Vision office and said to its leadership, "Get Tsehay." That was easier said than done and everyone knew it. Abductions are so common in the area that even the police are afraid of the guilty. They feel helpless and find it easier to ignore it than to fight for justice. It is a fight, they believe, they can never win. Everyone in the village knows this, including the World Vision staff. Even Tsehay's grandmother knew. But would that stop her? No. She would not take "never" for an answer. She wanted to find her beloved granddaughter and her only hope was the leadership team of World Vision. She was insistent.

Even though it seemed hopeless, the team agreed to try. Meanwhile, Tsehay was locked in a tiny room, held alone and in the dark night and day. She was given a small serving of doughy bread for sustenance. And she was repeatedly raped and suffered genital mutilation. She was in an unimaginable, unsustainable, intolerable, impossible situation. And she was there forty-five days, in a room barely big enough to move in.

But she was not alone. Before, during, and after the abductors came every day, she talked to God. She prayed. And, amazingly, she believed. It seemed impossible, but she prayed she could be released and kept asking God to let her go back to school—her greatest fear was she'd not be allowed to go to school. But she believed God would take care of her.

I'd guess her grandmother weighed less than one hundred pounds (by a long shot!). Nonetheless, she never stopped throwing her weight around. The World Vision staff held back. They didn't want to disappoint her by attempting the impossible and failing.

Have you ever known anyone to take a stand for righteousness and justice and to never ever back down? I know someone now, and it is Tsehay's grandmother. Finally, the two men on the leadership team of World Vision went to the police and insisted they try to find Tsehay. The men became part of the search squad.

Miraculously, Tsehay was found, rescued, and delivered from evil. Today she is bright-eyed, a wonderful student and right back on track with hope and a future. She never gave up. Neither did her mother or her stoic grandmother. Three generations of women believed that God was the safeguard of Tsehay. He covered her, even as she went through an unimaginable nightmare.

After we heard the whole story from her grandmother, speaking through the World Vision translator, Tsehay spoke up very softly. She said, "I can speak English. I understand you."

Everyone in that circle who spoke English cried even harder than we had been! In that moment, Tsehay and Jenna connected as though they were twins separated at birth. Jenna asked her interesting and wonderful questions about her life and Tsehay answered enthusiastically. We learned from her that she returned to class after missing "only" fifty-eight days and she is performing best in her eighth grade class. She said to us, "I will be an advocate for women's rights."

After more casual conversation, Jenna asked if she could pray for Tsehay. Before she prayed, Jenna, through her tears said, "Tsehay, those men wanted to give thirty dollars for you. Jesus gave so much more. He gave His life."

How many times do we find ourselves in an impossible situation, assuming there is no way out? We feel trapped by circumstances that vary from simply annoying to absolutely unmanageable. We feel stuck, and the word *impossible* comes to mind not just as an expression but as a feeling deep down inside. What do we do? Where do we turn? How do we manage the impossible?

Nothing in my life has ever come close to the story I heard standing on that hot, dusty, dry ground that was the grandmother's front yard. Even though I remember times I've felt battered, beaten, and alone, that's never happened to me physically. Jesus Himself said, "Lo, I am with you always. Even to the end of the age." Interesting how that truth was what held Tsehay safely in His grip, in spite of the torture she endured forty-five days and nights. It's the same truth that holds me in my challenging days and dark nights. While my challenges do not begin to compare to this young Ethiopian teenager's, what I need from my

Savior is very much the same. I need to know I am not alone. He is with me. I am safe in His grip regardless of the circumstances. And, this world is not my home, I'm just passing through. Our real treasures are not just in a different place but in a completely different realm.

Someday all who belong to Christ, from all over the world, will be joined with Him in an amazing ever-after where there will be no fear because there is nothing to fear; no pain because all will be perfect; no worry because our cares are left behind. I won't forget Tsehay, nor her mother and grandmother. I won't forget how, when they faced the impossible, they did not give up. Their suffering made them stronger. Hearing of their suffering somehow makes me stronger too. I won't forget, in my lowest moments, that I want to be as brave as Tsehay: "When you call on Jesus, *all* things are possible."

Little Is Much

® SANDI PATTY

Today I was making meat loaf, which is my absolute favorite "comfort" food. If I have been on the road a great deal, I will often come home and make my favorite home-cooked meal—meat loaf, baked potatoes with sour cream and butter, peas, and ice cream for dessert. I make my meat loaf a little differently: I use catsup, waffle syrup, mustard, and eggs as the sauce that you mix into the meat loaf. Then I glaze the top of the meat loaf with the same sauce, except for the eggs. It's fabulous—full of taste and spice and oh, so delicious.

As I was putting all the ingredients into the bowl, I began to pilfer through the spice cabinet and threw in some garlic, onions, pepper, and salt. I was looking for anything to literally spice it up. I couldn't imagine a bland, boring meat loaf without some added taste that only the spices can add. I mean, come on—meat loaf with no spice? Not workin' for me.

It may come as a surprise to some but I really, really love to cook. It's one of the things I love to do in my spare time. Whenever I get spare time, which isn't often, I really love to "throw down" a great meal for my family. And when I am cooking I do a lot of thinking. I think about the day I've had. I think about each of the kids, how they are, if they are doing okay. I think about the upcoming Women of Faith conference and how the audience will receive and respond to our messages this year. All that to say, I do a lot of thinking while I'm cooking.

So today, while making this wonderful comfort food, I was doing my usual thinking. But I began to think about the spices I was adding, especially the salt. You know, salt is a funny thing. If you add too much, it ruins the food. If you don't add enough, there isn't enough flavor. Matthew 5:13 came to mind: "You are the salt of the earth. But if the salt loses its saltiness, how can it be made salty again? It is no longer good for anything, except to be thrown out and trampled by men" (NIV).

When we visited Israel several years ago, we had the opportunity to go to the Red Sea, and we actually got to "swim" in the Red Sea. Now, the truth is, you don't really swim in the Red Sea because of all the salt—what you really do is float. You can't even try to sink to the bottom. The salt won't let you. All you do is float. It's pretty cool, actually. You just float along, kinda like you are on a raft of salt or something. You are safe from drowning and going under because of the salt.

So, if we are to be the salt of the earth, that requires much from us. There are many properties of salt besides just adding spice. Salt has the capacity to:

Preserve
Heal
Add flavor
Keep one afloat
Repel unwanted pests
Purify
Take away stains
Enhance taste

Salt is just a little grain, a tiny little fleck. And yet it can offer so much. It can be so much more than what it appears to be.

So how does that apply to our lives? Just imagine a kind word or a grace-giving gesture or a helpful action. A tiny deed, but it can help heal and keep someone afloat. It can purify and take away stains. It can soothe the wounds. Pretty powerful stuff can come from a very simple word or deed or action. To be the salt of the earth means to add something significant—not extravagant—to every situation. It means to live our lives striving to enhance each encounter or situation or relationship. To leave each encounter or situation or relationship better, full of life, more palatable.

I've always kind of skimmed over this verse before saying something like, "Yeah, yeah, salt, whatever." But as I began to really think about the properties of salt, I realized we have been called to no small task. Very often it's the very tasks that go unnoticed by the human eye, but so very noticed by the heavenly eyes, that mean the most.

Jesus often spoke of the little things that make enormous differences in people's lives—the mustard seed (Matt. 13:31–32), the widow's mite (Mark 12:41–44). Don't underestimate the power of little things. Little *is* much, when God is in it.

3

Seeing the Possibilities

LUCI SWINDOLL

There's nothing in the world like imagination. It is infinite—stretching the boundaries of time, circumstances, and resources. Picasso once said, "I am always doing things I can't do. That's how I get to do them." Don't you love that? I remember reading in one of my Picasso books that he wasn't afraid to invent *anything*. There was a big city dump near his home in the south of France, and he often went there to rummage through the pile, bringing home beat-up pieces of scrap metal, baskets, handlebars, cans, wheels, shovels, bottles, and all manner of trash, only to turn them into unforgettable and priceless sculptures. He said the form and texture of those pieces held the key to his imagination, as he saw a vision of each finished piece in his head before he ever left the junkyard.

Webster's Dictionary defines *imagination* as: "The action of forming mental images or concepts of what is not actually present to the senses; the faculty of producing ideal creations consistent with reality."

When I was an art major in college, one of my closest friends, Nancy Stewart, had a mind like Picasso's. She was superbly imaginative. Also an art major, she unconsciously drew people around her just to watch the work in progress. I questioned her ideas, explored out-of-the-way places with her to pick up scraps, or marveled with mutual friends over her unbelievable finished products. Nancy and I graduated the same year, and I well remember working on my final art piece for weeks in order to get it just right and turned in before the deadline, while Nancy did hers the night before with a big piece of wrapping paper and a can of shoe polish. I made a B+. She made an A. There was never any competition on my part though, because I was so mesmerized by her genuine and innate ability. I knew she was a creative genius and I was simply a young girl who loved and appreciated art. I sang her praises all the time and reveled in that unique skill to "form mental images of what is not present." And I was *never* disappointed.

After graduation, Nancy and I decided to share an apartment for a while. I was working as a draftsman-artist for Mobil Oil Corporation's Research Laboratory during the day and singing with the Dallas Opera at night. And she was teaching art at the local grade school. What a teacher she was! Every day she dreamed up something new for her students to enjoy and/or make with their hands. She wasn't afraid to let her imagination run wild.

One Saturday morning in December, the two of us were speeding along in her car ("The Green Bean," she called it—a long, green, ugly, sort-of-always-dirty Nash), chatting our heads off, when suddenly she made a U-turn right in the middle of the street and drove back to a big dumpster by a grocery store. Coming to a screeching halt, she jumped out, ran over to the dumpster and pulled out four huge pieces of cardboard. I'm sure they were once boxes, but had been cut apart and folded to get them at least part way down into the trash pile.

"What's up, Nancy?" I asked. "Are you gonna take these pieces of cardboard home? We can't even get them in the car. What are you gonna do with them?"

With complete nonchalance, she pulled them out of the dumpster, laid them on the ground, and walked around them several times, saying to me all the while, "There's a manger scene in here. I need one for my classroom this Christmas, and here it is. Wow! This is great."

Foolishly, I told her I didn't see any manger scene, to

which she replied, "Well, it's not there *yet*, but it will be. All I have to do is make it. I've been wondering where I was going to get one that'd be big enough, and when I saw this cardboard just lying there, it hit me—that's it!"

I knew better than to question her further, so we hauled these big pieces to The Green Bean, put them on top of the car, each holding our respective pieces out the window as tightly as possible to keep them from blowing off, and zigzagged down the road toward home. Nancy was beside herself. I can still see her in my mind's eye, laughing heartily at the prospect of her yet-to-be-built Christmas manger scene.

Within twenty-four hours, we had the little town of Bethlehem, baby Jesus lying in a manger, three wise men, the Virgin Mary, and dear Joseph, plus several animals, both standing and seated, in our small apartment. All it took was scissors, a craft knife, a yardstick, pencils, paint-brushes, four pieces of old, dirty cardboard . . . and several bushels of imagination!

Living with Nancy for those two years was a joy a minute. Every time I left the house I would say to her, "Listen, if you get the urge to make something while I'm gone, don't. Please wait 'til I get home so I can watch." If we had guests over for dinner, it wasn't enough just to ask them to come on a particular Saturday night or to set the table like normal folks. Oh no! We created invitations and printed them by hand, decorated the yard, made signs, designed place cards, draped the clothesline with paper vines and flowers, and served something we'd never cooked before. Everything was created from scratch, and the thrill of it was that Nancy knew beforehand exactly how it would turn out because she saw it in her head before it ever became a reality.

My friendship with Nancy opened my eyes and heart to numerous creative ideas I might not have ever tried, had I not seen her bring so many out-of-the-box creations to fruition. Just by being herself, and letting her God-given imagination be her guide, she rarely had a dull moment in life nor did anyone around her. Everyone marveled at this gift of seeing something finished before it was ever born.

I have two framed drawings by Nancy Stewart in my home—one is the head of Mozart and the other, Beethoven. They hang in my library among all my music books. I love those drawings and remember the day Nancy drew them. And, perhaps even more important, there's a small drawing that Nancy did of Maria Callas in the front of my 1959 program of the opera *Medea*. Nancy had gone to the performance with me one night while Callas was singing the lead and I was a member of the chorus. And while watching the opera, she sketched this little pencil drawing. I'm sure she had no idea I'd tape it inside that program cover and save it for fifty years.

And ironically, by that picture is a small handwritten note from me to Nancy that says, "*I just finished building a model city of Jerusalem. Very clever, abstract, and colorful. It started out as two huge flat sheets that had to be constructed and is in six levels. Took me three days to make it!*" (Who knows when *that* was written?) But by it is a response from her, "*Diane sent me The Globe Theater from London. Let's put it together!*"

Nancy taught me well. To this day, I build things all the time. Sometimes I have a pattern; sometimes I don't. Sometimes I know what to do when I start out; sometimes I don't. But the joy lies in seeing the possibilities in my head before I ever draw it out on paper. There's no telling what can be achieved when we simply begin even though we don't know in advance how it will turn out. The excitement lies in the invention.

Don't be afraid of imagination. It can be an endless source of amusement and entertainment. It's the powerhouse that supplies the mysterious force we call "inspiration." There are many opportunities that offer you a premade, premeasured, prepackaged life. But I encourage you not to settle for those. Dig into your own resources and see how much fun it is to step outside that and do your own thing. The author Leo Buscaglia wrote, "When your life seems emptier than it should, when it needs a healthy transfusion of vitality, use your imagination and tap your dreams." This is what Nancy did until the day she died. I'm so grateful to have known her and glad that I told her over and over what she meant to me and what her life and creativity meant to thousands.

If you find yourself bored with life, remember that with just a little imagination you can shake loose from that by making your moments creative, fresh, fun, different, and uniquely you.

> *Forcing yourself to use restricted means is the sort of restraint that liberates invention. It obliges you to make a kind of progress that you can't even imagine in advance.*
>
> — PABLO PICASSO, *In His Words*

4

An Over-the-Top Banquet

✍ SHEILA WALSH

> *Then I heard the sound of massed choirs, the sound of a mighty cataract, the sound of strong thunder: Hallelujah! The Master reigns, our God, the Sovereign-Strong! Let us celebrate, let us rejoice, let us give him the glory! The Marriage of the Lamb has come; his Wife has made herself ready. She was given a bridal gown of bright and shining linen. The linen is the righteousness of the saints. The Angel said to me, "Write this: 'Blessed are those invited to the Wedding Supper of the Lamb.'"*
>
> —REVELATION 19:6–9 MSG

When I left college at twenty-one I joined the music department of European Youth for Christ. I was part of a music group called Oasis, and we toured all over Europe singing in schools and colleges. One of the most interesting aspects of that time was that rather than stay in hotels, we stayed with local volunteers in each city. I had enough high school French to squeak through our time in France and the French part of Switzerland but I was simply sunk in Germany and Holland. Most of the time, we would have a translator with us for the initial introductions, and then we would just survive on hand signals. That worked pretty well until I stayed with a family in Holland who were convinced that if they talked to me often enough and loud enough I would by some linguistic miracle understand them.

On my first evening in their home the lady asked me, at quite an impressive volume, something that sounded like, "Vooter tooter trooter?" (No disrespect intended to the fine people of Holland.) I smiled and nodded only to realize that I had just been asked if I would like two boiled eggs and some toast. I can't stomach boiled eggs—they make me sick—but our Youth for Christ rulebook said that we had to eat what was put in front of us and not offend our hosts. I wasn't sure what would be more offensive, refusing boiled eggs or barfing on her lovely rug. Somehow I kept them down, I am sure, by the grace of God.

On my final day with this lovely family, the mother grasped me by my arm as I was heading upstairs to get my suitcase. She stared into my eyes and with a big smile said, "Hooten . . ." well, you know roughly how the rest goes. I assumed she was giving me a final blessing as I headed off. I assumed wrong. When I came downstairs with a case that was groaning like an over-indulgent diner at an all-you-can-eat breakfast bar, she handed me a large trash bag. Inside were all the things that no longer fit her—sweaters, dresses, and large Dutch bras! I couldn't refuse, so I had to drag that bag with me all the way to Denmark where I dropped it off at a homeless shelter and quickly left.

Touring in England should have been a breeze after that, but surprisingly, some of my greatest challenges were with English families. Once I stayed with a family one very cold December weekend, and after we'd had a cup of tea I excused myself and asked if I might go to bed as we had an early start the next morning. The lady of the house asked her husband to take his car out of the garage. I thought to myself, "How sweet. They are putting me in a hotel." Instead the husband drove the car out, and the wife set up a cot in the garage. It was *so* cold. I put more clothes on to go to bed than I had been wearing all day. I even longed for the big Dutch bras, as they might have kept my ears warm! Every thirty minutes the chest freezer would roar into action like a beast in a Friday-night horror movie. Ah, the joys of life on the road.

I have tasted *interesting* food in many countries, but I don't think anything, other than perhaps an Indiana Jones movie, could have prepared me for Bangkok, Thailand. I was on a tour of Southeast Asia, singing in universities, churches, and U.S. army bases. When I arrived in Bangkok my host asked if I would like to eat at a typical Thai restaurant. Well, I've had Thai food here at home, so I said that would be lovely. I discovered that day that Thai food in Thailand is very different than Thai food in America. There were eight of us at dinner—six locals, a young missionary from Texas, and me. My host offered to order for me, as the menu was in Thai, and I thanked him for doing that.

The first dish to arrive was soup. I say it was soup because the missionary from Texas told me it was soup. No self-respecting Scottish woman would ever refer to this dish as soup. It was black and had things floating in it. I whispered to one of my companions, "What are the things floating in it?" to which she replied, "Don't ask. You really don't want to know." Turns out my training didn't include a prayer to cover this kind of soup. So I tried to mentally go to a happy place and forced most of it down. I have now ruined that happy place forever. (I lived to discover that it was lung, bladder, and intestine soup and, no, I don't have the recipe.)

Although I've had many meals on the road that tested and strengthened my prayer life, I have also received some amazing hospitality on the road and made many friendships that have lasted to this day. There is something about the very act of sitting down together over a meal that seems almost sacred. It was an important element of Christ's life and the final thing that he did with his friends before enduring the pain of crucifixion. As a family, we have chosen to make dinnertime count. Some nights it would be so easy to just plunk ourselves down in front of the TV and stare as we eat, but we try to do that very rarely. Instead we sit and eat and talk together. It seems that when children get to a certain age, it's often the only opportunity to connect with them about their day. During the out-of-school, summer months we buy a new cookbook, and at least one night a week we cook a meal together. Christian enjoys learning and I'm thinking this will pay off one day for his future wife. We've had very successful meals and ones that left a little to be desired, but either way we've had fun.

But no matter how delicious any meal we share on this earth, nothing will compare with the feast we will celebrate together with the Lamb of God. I can't imagine what will be served, can you? I'm sure there will be flavors, textures, and aromas we have never encountered before. Everything will be pure perfection and nothing will be fattening. But more precious and enjoyable than the food will be seeing His face. We will finally see Jesus face-to-face. I can only imagine.

> *This is the hour of banquet and of song;*
> *This is the heavenly table spread for me;*
> *Here let me feast, and feasting, still prolong*
> *The hallowed hour of fellowship with Thee.*
> *Here would I feed upon the bread of God,*
> *Here drink with Thee the royal wine of Heaven;*
> *Here would I lay aside each earthly load,*
> *Here taste afresh the calm of sin forgiven.*
>
> —HORATIUS BONAR, 1855

5

Bread in Africa

 NICOLE C. MULLEN

A couple of years ago I was asked to go to Ghana, West Africa, with an organization that dealt with freeing an enslaved group of women called *trokosi*, meaning "slaves to the gods." In the practice of *trokosi*, young girls, often as young as five years old, are given to local priests as living human sacrifices, their lives expected to atone for their families' sins. They are modern-day slaves, forced to work long days in the fields and forbidden from attending school. They are trapped, along with any children they may have, in a life of servitude.

I felt it was important to take my newly teenage daughter along for the experience, so with much prayer and great excitement, we took off for an adventure across the sea for her first trip to Africa. Upon our arrival in

Ghana, we quickly learned that the people were naturally beautiful, the roads were sometimes paved but were mostly dirt, and that our surroundings would be a mixture of modern and rural. Our hosts were very warm and self-sacrificing, frequently going out of their way to make us comfortable. They explained the culture, answered our questions, and interpreted conversations for us.

Soon we were taken to meet some of the ladies and girls who were once enslaved in *trokosi* and had a chance to hear their stories firsthand. Then we drove to and resided at their vocational training center for a couple of days, a place that keeps a long waiting list. It is there that these newly freed women are now learning how to economically provide for themselves, learning how to dye fabrics, make dresses, bake, and create soaps, balms, and lotions. After graduating from the two-year course, the women are given a fresh start and are set up with the tools that they will need to begin their new businesses.

One of my favorite moments of the trip came one day as we headed out for a village where several of the graduates worked together and set up shop in the marketplace. We purchased fine dyed cloths and handmade soaps for bathing and washing clothes. The women were so excited that we came. Their items were priced at the equivalent of U.S. cents, but the quality was high. Not to mention that it was truly organic. So of course, we bought a lot. Then we moved on to the outdoor bakery. The wonderful scent of bread filled the air and our senses—the smell alone would have made one's stomach growl. So again we bought and bought.

It was then that we noticed that, in the midst of the abundance of delicious bread, there were many hungry children gathered around us—some of them the children of the bakers. Though their mothers were the ones making and selling the bread, the children knew that they could not freely eat of it. The ingredients to make the bread had cost money, and the only way to make a profit would be to sell it, and not to eat it. And so the little ones just watched.

Just as Jesus was once faced with a hungry crowd and had compassion on them and did something to meet their needs, we, too, felt compelled to feed these children. Looking around at the faces of the hungry brown angels standing in front of us, we prepared to take the bread and bless it, break it, and share it. Because of the language barrier, I didn't know how to tell the kids that this bread was purchased for them.

And so, without ceremony, I broke off a piece of bread and offered it to one of the children before me, along with the words "God bless you." The child in turn responded back to me with a smile and his version of the same phrase: "Goblesho." Soon, there were children and out-stretched hands all around me. One of our hosts, who spoke their language, told the children to line up neatly in front of me or they wouldn't get any bread. Wow, what an overwhelming response that brought: they lined up *fast*. I must admit that I thought the children might be a little put out by my offering them the very thing that their own mothers had made. But they understood they could only eat the bread if someone first paid the price for it. Otherwise, to eat it without payment would mean the end of their business, which could mean starvation for many.

So we purchased all the bread they had. With a heart full of joy, I quietly blessed it, carefully broke it, and hap-pily shared it. As the verbal volley of "God bless you" and "Goblesho" continued, I noticed that I was starting to run low on the loaves. I began to pray harder and tear the pieces into smaller chunks. Though on my face I wore a smile, inside I was pleading with God to multiply what was in my hands, as he did in the Bible. I reminded him of the times he did the same thing when he walked the earth. The time when he was surrounded by five thou-sand hungry men, not including their wives and children, and he did not have the heart to send them away with their bellies empty. So he asked his friends, his disciples, how much food they had to share with the people. They had nothing of their own to give but returned with only a small boy's lunch of five loaves of bread and two fish. I'm sure at least some of them must have thought that Jesus would probably say, "What am I supposed to do with this? Is this a joke or something?" Or maybe they were hoping that he would say, "OK, you guys are right, let's just send them away so that we can get some rest and find some food for ourselves."

Instead, Jesus told them to tell the people to sit down on the grass in groups of fifties and hundreds. This meant they were going to be there for a while. The disciples must have been a little upset, because this was supposed to have been a vacation for them. They had been traveling for a while and working with crowds of people everywhere they went, and compassion was probably not what they were feeling at that moment. Still, Jesus took the little that had been given him, blessed it, broke it, and then charged his friends with sharing it. By the miracle he performed, they had so much food that everyone ate until they were full, and they still had twelve baskets filled with what remained.

After remembering this, I whispered, "He's the same yesterday, today and forever," along with other scriptures and promises that came to mind. I was asking for help, and a present-day miracle for the least of these. Still, the bread was dwindling as the line of children in front of me did not appear to be doing the same. Eventually, I came to the last piece and didn't have the heart to split it in half again, lest my offering to the child in front of me appear too small. So with a shrug of my shoulders, I raised up my empty hands and showed the kids who were still in line that I had no more bread. I did not have enough.

The children didn't pout, or look at me angrily, but seemed to accept this lack as their way of life. I hugged the little ones around me, fought back tears, and made my way to the bus, feeling a little bit defeated. But before I could settle into my seat beside my daughter, someone who was already aboard the bus announced that we still had extra loaves under the seat that had been purchased from an earlier site, and I could use those to feed the rest of the kids. I was so excited! I remembered thanking God over and over again. He had heard me in Africa, and he had once again provided.

That day we had more than enough bread. Every child who wanted some got some, and then some. I left with my heart full, and my faith strengthened. I am continually amazed at how God shows himself as The Champion time and time again. He proves that nothing is too difficult for him, and that he works on his own timetable and not mine. Who's to say that, had I left that day without more bread for the kids, God would not have still provided through another source? He most certainly could have done that, and looking back, I firmly believe that he would have. But it was so kind of him to let me witness his love in action.

The bread I passed out to the kids that day would not sustain them for a lifetime, but the bread he fed me will. And I believe that the pronouncement of a blessing over those kids, as simple as it was, may be the seeds that he allows to grow into something grand in their lives. Though he takes pleasure in meeting our physical needs, he is far more concerned about our spiritual ones because he knows that the inside of a man will last eons beyond the outer shell that we walk around in. His aim is to woo us for eternity. And just like the bread that had to be paid for so that those little brown angels could eat it, so Jesus paid the price for us to have fellowship with God. He himself became the bread that was blessed, broken, and now shared. He is offered to all who will receive him.

So, eat abundantly and "Goblesho!"

6

A Garden Worth Tending

◆ PATSY CLAIRMONT

Your wife shall be like a fruitful vine
In the very heart of your house,
Your children like olive plants
All around your table.

—Psalm 128:3

I am always amazed, when I haven't seen my married friends and their families for a time, and then we get together, how their children have grown. That's often how reality slaps me silly. I question, how can that much time have gone by? Then I inch past a mirror and think, "Uh, oh, it definitely has."

There's something about growth that's eye-catching, possibly startling, and usually stunning. It's what we were created for. We are designed and called to growth. Not just growing old, but growing up. Growing old we have no control over, trust me I've tried sidestepping it. While growing up, maturing, relies on our willing participation, if not our absolute relinquishment.

Recently I've been studying and exploring vines, vineyards, and fruit. In my quest to learn more I discovered several things I think you might find interesting. I was wide-eyed and attentive as the keeper of a vineyard I visited, shared with me.

To begin with, he told me that when you look for productive vines the leaves tell a story. Really happy leaves signify the vine has put all its energy into showiness and doesn't have enough life left to give to the fruit. Whereas leaves that are almost wilted have concentrated their life-energy into the fruit that it might produce bountifully.

Now that would preach. It's all about priorities, passion, and productivity. It's easy to want; it's another thing entirely to work. For instance, I want to grow as a writer and be fruitful, but that requires tremendous concentration and dedication. In other words, w-o-r-k.

The big green leaves of my wishing don't make it happen. It's when I sacrifice something I really want to do and dedicate that time to my writing that I begin to see growth in my efforts and fruit in the outcome. In other words, if I give up the unfruitful pastime of talking about becoming a writer with a crisper pen and begin the life-bearing tasks of actually pressing the pen against the paper, results will follow.

I am impressed when I read about great writers and the time, education, financial investment, and other kinds of sacrificial effort it took them to develop in their craft. Yet while I am impressed I can't say I'm eager or even capable of locking myself away from my family and the world to take the next steps in development. I'm a rather social gal and certainly a family one.

Yet I do think there are hours I could redeem for writing that wouldn't interfere with time I spend loving on and being loved by others. I could give up a few television shows (I'm an HGTV junkie), cut back on Facebook time, and use airport and flying time to my writing advantage. Of course, this means discipline because changing habits is not easy, and giving up things I enjoy feels wilting. But, hey, like we just read, wilting is good if it leads to fruitfulness. (I wonder how many times I'll need to repeat that before it's a recorded message on my speed dial.)

When I go through the airports, which is almost weekly, I have favorite places I love to visit and spots I enjoy stopping to eat. And I have an addictive habit of treating myself to a new home magazine to peruse during flight, a bag of dark chocolate M&M's, and a blueberry muffin to nibble on. Just think of the hidden time, not to mention calories, I could redeem just by rearranging my priorities.

Speaking of nibbling and hiding, what about dieting? Ugh. We all know we can talk a good weight loss program, but implementing it is a whole other lettuce leaf. I'm almost certain I could ruffle my leaves and tell you how you could lose weight, while I sit, fill out, and lap over the cushion on my own sofa.

Yep, if there's no fruit the leaf is just a showy story . . . all pomp, no profit.

I also learned from the vine keeper that the roses that grow in close proximity to the vines serve a purpose other than their beauty. (What good news for us beauty queens!) The rosebushes are susceptible to the same diseases as the grapevines, only the roses being more delicate in design are affected first. So the roses serve as a warning to the vine keepers of how to protect their fields.

Roses . . . what lovely guards. What a fragrant picture. Of course they must be peripheral in their presence lest they affect the flavor of the fruit. So they surround the field in a bit of distant glory.

The roses remind me of the Holy Spirit's ever-present protective work for our benefit. The Holy Spirit, while central in our lives, does not tout Himself but always lifts up Jesus. The Spirit's glory is peripheral to His message of our Savior. And the resulting work of the Holy Spirit is emitted through the fragrant results of what He teaches us. The Spirit acts as our Rose Guard alerting us to dangers that can disturb the roots of our faith and diminish the fruit. He speaks His concerns to our spirit via conviction and during prayer conversations.

Another truth. Did you know in some areas that grapevines cannot flourish in the soil and so other vines that respond well are planted in their stead? I was told by the experts that when the roots are firmly established the grapevine is then grafted in, allowing it to grow and flourish out of the healthy base.

Is that not a picture of those of us who come to Christ? He by His finished work on Calvary grafts us, when we give our lives to Him, into His family. Christ is the vine and we are the branches, which gives us the privilege of bearing and holding the fruit until harvest. Fruitfulness is the result of abiding (dwelling in) in the life-producing flow of Christ's life.

The vine keeper told me that during the growing season his men go out and trim off many of the newly forming grapes to ensure the other grapes are strong. It would appear heartless or wasteful yet purposeful pruning is necessary to produce a fine crop.

Likewise God, who guides the husbandry, selectively

cuts back in our lives so that we might produce righteousness. The lopping off of branches cuts into our own plans at times, but it is always done with a final outcome in mind.

Some years ago my husband bought a super-duper riding lawn mower. Les could hardly wait to try out his new toy—excuse me, his new equipment. He even bought a spiffy hat for his maiden voyage, so Les was looking good. He revved up the powerful motor, careened out the garage door, onto the grass, where he lowered the mower, shifted into high gear, and proceeded to barrel right through my flower bed.

That was not what Les meant to do. That was not what I wanted him to do. By the time Les lifted the mower and made his way out of the flowers, my hydrangea bush looked like a handful of pickup sticks, my roses were potpourri, and my butterfly bush was not fit for a gnat. This was not purposeful pruning at its best.

Even so, would you believe the following year those bushes came back with gusto? They were full of gorgeous blossoms. And the year after that they were show stoppers. Folks were actually stopping to take pictures of them.

It's really a reminder that what others do accidentally or spitefully can be used to cause us to flourish. Doesn't that remind you of Joseph from Genesis? If you remember, his life looked like nothing but hardship and injustice. From sibling jealousy, to female revenge, to ingratitude, Joseph's story looked like he had been mowed down and discarded. But God used it all as pruning to cause Joseph to grow into a wise leader.

None of us would volunteer for family rejection, slavery, imprisonment, or injustice. When Joseph was young and still full of innocent dreams, he never imagined as the favored child of his father he would live such a rootless existence. But God grafted him into the Egyptian world for holy purposes of position and provision. Joseph, after being cut down like a sapling, grew to become an oak of righteousness. His management of the fruit of the fields flourished the people through a world famine.

We can observe growth in a petrie dish, a preschool, and a seniors vocational center. We were born to grow until our fruit falls to earth for the last time and we blossom into eternal life.

I am the true vine, and My Father is the vinedresser.

—JOHN 15:1

7

Are You There?

MARILYN MEBERG

Years ago Ken and I saw a movie entitled *Are You There?* It was one of those kinds of movies I loved and Ken endured. It centered on an elderly British woman whose paranoia and insecurities about life as well as personal safety caused her much angst. Every few minutes she would stealthily creep to her front door, open it a crack, and peer through the small opening, whispering, "Are you there?" Then she would quickly shut the door. The camera would blur and the lights dim; Ken would groan and do some whispering of his own: "Surely this whole movie is not going to be a picture of her shrouded face behind a door; seeing only one eyeball gives me the creeps!"

I, of course, was consumed by the somber lighting, quiet cello background music, and the curiosity of who the woman thought might be "there." Who was she waiting for, and why? Will that person ever appear and, if so, will the woman's face register relief? Will she then invite the person to walk through the door and enter her home? If she does, is that a wise decision? What might the consequences be?

For months after seeing this movie, I would spook Ken by lurking about the house and periodically whispering, "Are you there?" He never failed to give a gratifying response. Sometimes he was uncertain, vague, or noncommittal. But my favorite response was when he grabbed me unexpectedly from behind a closet door and croaked in my ear, "I'm here."

Is there not something poignantly universal about asking the question "Are you there?" Since the beginning of time, human beings have been curious about what's "out there." For eons pagan civilizations have prayed to the moon, the stars, or the sun in an effort to connect with a wished-for deity. With each prayer was the wistful, "Are you there?"

The very God who made the moon, stars, sun, and all other created things quietly came to this planet two thousand years ago for the express purpose of saying, "Yes . . . I am here." Jeremiah 29:13–14 assures us this God, this Jesus, the Son of God, is here and can be found: "If you look for me in earnest, you will find me when you seek me. I will be found by you" (NLT).

I heard an amazing testimony of this "you will find me" promise from a young woman who had come to our Women of Faith Friday feature. Sandi Patty, Steve Arterburn, and I did the Friday feature last year, and Dr. Henry Cloud came for several weeks to fill in for Steve who was on "maternity leave." During one of the Henry Cloud dates I noticed a woman sitting alone in the VIP section. I went over to introduce myself to her, and she told me her name was Helene and she was a friend of Henry's. She had come that morning to hear him. I welcomed her and then nursed my "did not come to hear you" feelings back to my own chair next to Henry's. He grinned at my telling of the brief encounter and said, "Wait till you hear her story, Marilyn . . . it is phenomenal." Later, over lunch, I learned her story.

She had heard Henry say on the *New Life Live* radio show that God is one who can be found and one who can be known. Having told a caller who wondered how to find God to simply ask him to show himself and give his name, Henry told the caller, "God will hear you; you will find him."

Helene heard that radio show and decided to "try it" for herself. She had just received a cancer diagnosis and was devastated. She got down on her knees and simply said, "If there is anybody out there . . . help me. Whoever you are, if there is a God, just please help me."

As Henry heard her account some time later, he asked Helene what happened. She said it was hard to describe but that it was as if she were surrounded in a warm, peaceful, loving bubble. She said she was literally engulfed in it and that she knew it was Jesus who was there; he told her she would be okay. Then, after a brief period of time, he left.

Those of us at the lunch table who heard this story felt awed by it but startled when she said the whole experience was really a problem for her. She had asked for God and got Jesus instead. I looked at Henry, who was smiling warmly throughout this narrative. We all wanted to know why it was a problem to "get Jesus instead of God." She said, "Because I'm Jewish!!" I dropped my fork. Mercy! How creative of the God of the universe to present himself in such a tenderly personal fashion!

In his book *The Secret Things of God*, Henry writes of the supreme privilege he had talking Helene through the many Old Testament scriptures with which she was familiar but had never connected to Jesus: the Passover, the Lamb, the sacrifices, and how the Jews knew the coming Messiah would be the Passover Lamb. That Lamb would be called Immanuel, which means "God with us." Helene came to understand that Jesus was the one who fulfilled all those prophecies. Henry helped her see what she had experienced in her initial prayer was exactly what God wanted her to understand and why she, as a Jew, needed to meet Jesus!

Most of us do not have the personal drama God ordained for Helene as he provided a way for her to find Jesus, the sacrificial Lamb, and connect that finding with the God who is there. But scripture is clear: God is available. He says, "Those who diligently seek me will find me" (Proverbs 8:17 NASB).

I think it would be wise for us to take a moment here to discuss an unacceptable human motive that may cause some to "seek God": that motive for seeking is not pure. For example, the seeking prayer that demands God show himself in some tangible and miraculous way and, if he does not, the seeker says, "OK, I'm done with you. You didn't show up and do what I asked, so I don't believe you exist!" That kind of prayer is manipulative. Insisting God do some kind of "performance trick" in order to win the seeker over to belief is not truly seeking him. That thinking and seeking reduces God to a circus animal that barks on demand.

Satan, the sworn enemy of God and of us his people, tried to reduce Jesus to doing a "performance trick." We read in Matthew 4 how Satan told Jesus to jump off the highest point of the temple and then to call for the protection of angels who would prevent him from injury. Jesus' response was, "The Scriptures also say, 'Do not test the Lord your God'" (v. 7 NLT). When a seeker demands performance tricks from God as a prerequisite for belief, the seeker is guilty of the very kind of testing Satan tried with Jesus. When Helene cried out to God, not knowing if he was truly there, her heart was seeking to know him. Her motive was pure. Her personal anguish that led her to seek God was genuine. And then God gave her more than she could ever ask or think.

The compelling truth about God is that he wants a relationship with his creation. If any one of his created ones seeks to know him and, genuinely seeks to find Him, he is always there! First Timothy 2:4 clearly states that God "wants everyone to be saved and to understand the truth" (NLT). What is that truth? Jesus said, "I am the way and the truth and the life. No one comes to the Father except through me. If you really knew me, you would know my Father as well. From now on, you do know him and have seen him" (John 14:6–7 NIV).

Perhaps you have seen the nineteenth-century painting entitled *The Light of the World*. In it Christ is seen holding a lantern standing outside a little cottage on a dark and stormy night. He is knocking on the door of the home, waiting to be invited in. The depiction of Jesus is seen bathed in a golden light. It appears as if he is prepared to stand outside the door knocking for as long as it takes. Were any one of us to crack the door open and peering out ask the question, "Are you there?" the answer is and will always be, "Yes, I am here. I will be here for all eternity if you wish. All you have to do is open the door and invite me in."

Part 2

8

Imagine That!

SHEILA WALSH

No one's ever seen or heard anything like this, never so much as imagined anything quite like it—what God has arranged for those who love him.

—1 Corinthians 2:9 msg

There are moments in life that stand out because they are breathtakingly beautiful. There are moments that stay with us because they are painful beyond belief. There are also those moments that are scratched into our memories because we think, *I can't believe that just happened!* This story is about one of those moments.

I was almost finished writing one of my very first books, and the discussion on the table was about the cover. I will refrain from mentioning the title in case any of those involved in that little "adventure" don't see the funny side in all of this. My book company wanted to go with a photograph of me on the front, as I was not a very well-known author. My thought was, *Why put a photo of me on the cover if people don't know who I am—that would only seem to confirm it!* But my manager at the time agreed with my publisher, and so I lost and a photo shoot was set up. I asked my manager if I could see any of the photos that the photographer had previously taken. He said he thought that he may have taken a photo of Dolly Parton on a motorbike but couldn't come up with any physical evidence! I asked about the makeup and hair artist and was assured that she had a wonderful reputation around town. (*For what?* I wondered.)

Well, the day arrived and I showed up at the studio at 9 a.m. to start hair and makeup. The receptionist directed me to the makeup room and told me the name of the makeup artist; I will call her Florence. She seemed like a very sweet lady, in her mid-fifties. I told her that I would get some coffee and give her some time to set up. She told me that she had set up. Well, how best to describe the makeup displayed before me? My immediate thought was, *I think Mother Teresa has a bigger makeup kit than this.* There was one color of foundation, powder, pink lipstick, and blue eye shadow—I kid you not! She suggested that she start with my hair and I sat down, wondering what she might come up with. When she pulled out a bag of small foam rollers, I had a clue. I remembered those rollers. When I was a teenager I used to do my mom's hair every Friday night. I would shampoo and condition it in the kitchen sink then roll it up in small pink rollers. It seemed I was about to receive my very own version of the much-loved shampoo and set!

I asked Florence if she had any larger rollers, but she assured me that these had never failed her yet. Once she had all my hair trapped, she started on my makeup. I decided that the only way to take my mind off what was going on was to get to know her a little bit. We chatted and swapped stories about our families. It was clear to me that she was a very sweet woman who was bringing the best she had to the table that day. She said to me, "I hope you are happy with what I do—I take my job very seriously."

At that moment my manager popped his head round the door and got his first look at the new me. I don't think he could have looked more horrified if I had been sitting there bald with a dead raccoon on my head. Fortunately, Florence couldn't see him. I asked her if she could give us a couple of minutes to chat about the shoot, so she slipped out to get a soda. I said to him, "Look, I realize that I look like a trucker's bad date but there is no point in saying anything. She is a sweet lady and she is giving me the best she has. If I thought she had options, we could have some input, but this is it. Trust me, we will laugh about this later—much later."

I knew we would have to do a new shoot, so I just decided to have a good time with this one. I thought, *How much worse could it get?* Then I met the photographer. He was very friendly and warm and told me that he wanted me to feel as at home and comfortable as possible. We'll call him Frank. He suggested that we start with me sitting on a stool. I got myself as comfortable as only a trucker's bad date can get, and told him that I was ready. After a few adjustments to the lighting and a few test Polaroids, he picked up his camera and a small toy mouse on the end of a long stick and began to shoot. Yes, I said small toy mouse on the end of a stick. Before every shot he wagged the mouse in my face and made what I assumed were supposed to be encouraging noises. I handled about two minutes of this before I had to ask.

"Frank, I don't mean to be rude here, but can you tell me why you are waving that thing in my face?"

Frank was obviously confused by the question, which finally made sense when he told me that he usually photographs cats. Apparently he was a part-time clown and part-time cat photographer. Trust me, you can't make this stuff up.

When I finally got the photos back, it happened to be on a day when I was having lunch with one of my best friends, so I said to her, "OK, I need you to work with me here. I want you to imagine the worst photograph of me that you have ever seen and then multiply it by twenty. When I show you this photo, tell me how close you came to what you're about to see."

When I showed her the pictures, I thought I might have had to call 911, as my friend seemed unable to breathe.

"So how close did you come?" I asked.

"Not within a million miles," she replied when she was finally able to talk. "Not within a million miles!"

Do you know that moment waits for you and for me? Now I don't mean the shock of seeing a friend displayed in bright-blue eye shadow and tight curls. I do mean that there is a day coming for those of us who love and trust Jesus that we can't even begin to conjure up in our minds. That's quite a shocking promise. Think about it. Hollywood is able to produce some amazing special effects, and add to that we all have pretty vivid imaginations—but even in our wildest dreams we won't come even close to what God has prepared for us. I wonder if it's because everything we see and hear will be new or if everything we see and hear will be beyond what we could have imagined—pure, free, and perfect. I can't imagine something so breathtaking that the thought of it hasn't even entered into my mind, but I guess that's the whole point.

When Paul wrote this letter to the church in Corinth, he was writing to a community very much on the cutting edge of everything new. He had spent eighteen months with them as their pastor, showing them how to live and love one another before he moved on to other churches that needed his help. Then he received news that they were losing hold of what was true and grasping for new supernatural experiences.

Paul wrote to encourage them to hold on to the truth, but he gave them a promise to hold on to as well. He wrote to them, just as to us, to remind us that there is a day coming when no matter what man can conjure up, it will not hold a candle to what God had prepared for those who love him. Imagine that!

9

Lift High Your Glass

LUCI SWINDOLL

Several months ago I read Peggy Noonan's wonderful little book *On Speaking Well*, published in 1998 and loaded with timeless ideas for any speaker, anywhere. The subtitle is "How to Give a Speech with Style, Substance, and Clarity." Being a Women of Faith speaker, I grabbed that book off the shelf once I knew it existed . . . and read it from cover to cover. Peggy Noonan is one of the finest speechwriters in the nation. She's written for Presidents Bush and Reagan and has extensive practical advice for those of us who stand before the public, delivering information we trust is relevant, important, and engaging. The opening quote by Roscoe Drummond grabbed me right off the bat: "The mind is a wonderful thing. It starts working the minute you're born and never stops until you get up to speak in public."

Ain't it the truth? Something in us stops functioning when we're in front of other people, trying to tell them something as a group. All of us have had that feeling. We're embarrassed. Uncomfortable. Cautious. Intimidated. Why? Because we try too hard. We want everything to be perfect, and if it's not, we're afraid the audience will hate us and run us out of town. Trust me, they won't. I've been imperfect almost every time I've opened my mouth in public and I'm still speaking. I've so appreciated Peggy's comment: "Don't be so eager to be bright and quick and clever and memorable. Be you, try to be honest, speak with all the candor you can muster and say it the way you'd say it to your family." I'm memorizing that quote!

One of the finest chapters in the book is on giving toasts and tributes. Who writes on *that*? Nobody! But Peggy Noonan develops the topic in such a convincing way; it makes the reader want to be invited to write a toast every day.

Did you know there's a toast in the Bible? A toast to God. It's in Psalm 116 and it's beautiful. The primary thought of the chapter revolves around King David's praising God for his deliverance from death. He's thanking God for hearing his cry for mercy. When David was overcome with trouble and sorrow, he called on the name of the Lord. With graciousness and compassion God heard his cry and saved him. God kept his eyes from tears, his feet from stumbling, and his soul from death, so King David lifts his voice and his cup in gratitude. Verses 12 through 14 read: "What can I give back to GOD for the blessings he's poured out on me? I'll lift high the cup of salvation—a toast to God! I'll pray in the name of GOD; I'll complete what I promised GOD I'd do, and I'll do it together with his people" (MSG).

Since I was a little girl, I've loved toasts. The first one I remember was one given by my father at a Christmas dinner when our family and various guests were present. Although I was young, I thought it was so . . . I don't know . . . *cool*. Kind. Thoughtful. Daddy was honoring someone who'd been ill throughout that year, had surgery, and had finally overcome the odds. He was seated at our table. We all raised our water glasses as we toasted this gentleman, thanking God for his restored health. It made an indelible impression on me. Because I so adored my dad, I wanted to be like him. I wanted to be a good "toast-giver," like he was—one who could focus on others in an honoring way, with his words.

Most of us are scared to be asked to give a toast— fearful we'll stutter, say something stupid, or drop our glass. And standing in front of other people just makes it worse. But let me encourage you to step up to the plate and give it your best shot. Here are a few pointers that might help:

BE SINCERE. Sometimes we think we have to be funny or clever to the point of being flippant. When we're sincere, we are giving a gift to the person we're toasting. And if what we say happens to be funny, that's the bow on the gift . . . not the gift itself. Also, it doesn't have to be deeply profound, if we're sincere. When we've been asked to be the toastmaster, it's because we have a deep affection for the person we're toasting.

BE BRIEF. Nothing is gained by droning on and on forever, saying little while trying to be witty. Our job is to capture a moment in time. We're summing up a contribution and the meaning of that contribution to those in the room or the city, or (in some cases) the world. When we think through what we want to say, the toast may be the most meaningful thing that happens at the dinner party, or the gala. And the words, though brief, will live forever because they were sincere and to the point, in high praise of the one receiving the tribute.

BE YOURSELF. There is a multitude of words and thoughts that can be used to honor another individual, but when we choose the ones that come from our own hearts, there's nothing better. The poet e. e. cummings once wrote in a letter to a friend: "To be nobody but your-self in a world which is doing its best, night and day, to make you everybody else means to fight the hardest bat-tle which any human being can fight; and never stop fighting." We all want to hear from people who are origi-nal—with original thoughts, ideas, and style. You be that person.

Last year Marilyn Meberg turned seventy. A group of her friends and family gave her a bang-up-big-time party. We planned a magnificent dinner at a local, elegant res-taurant with thirty-five of her favorite people present, from eight different states: Texas, Michigan, Florida, Oklahoma, California, Ohio, Indiana, and Tennessee. The evening included a beautiful birthday cake made by a gifted chef who is also an employee at Women of Faith; floral arrangements from Petals (Marilyn's favorite flower shop); a menu chosen and designed by one of Marilyn's closest friends; a program emceed by Mary Graham with sketches acted out by Marilyn's children; and decorations with place cards on each table from yours truly. My brother Chuck offered the blessing. I can't even tell you how fun and exciting it was to plan and execute all those festivities in Marilyn's honor.

Yet, with all of this, one of the most memorable

moments of the evening was the *toast*. That was the very first thing given. It was written by Women of Faith's resident dramatist, Nicole Johnson. With everyone's glass lifted high, the toast was read as we paid tribute to Marilyn. Let me share it with you.

A Toast to Marilyn

What an auspicious occasion on which to raise a glass. Note the alacrity with which we rise in your honor. From all of us "sweet babies" we toast your life and the propitious impact it has had on us, which is inestimable.

For expanding our vocabulary in a multiplicity of ways,

For illuminating the amusing and helping us choose it for ourselves,

For demonstrating that through the "unzippering" of our hearts we can be whole people (or at least a good solid half if we try hard),

For being the tenderest shepherd of thousands of women seeking to make the decision of a lifetime,

For having the courage to add color to your commentary in a black-and-white world,

For championing the good news to all the abandoned, lonely hearts . . . like ours,

For the depth, the insight, the empathy, and the inspiration—we adore you and celebrate your celibacy, uhm your seventy, years on this earth!

Cheers, cheers, cheers!"[1]

Maybe it's never occurred to you to use a special occasion, or any occasion, to give a friend or family member a "shout out." Regardless of what's in your glass, think of who you're celebrating and give them one of the greatest gifts of all—words. Words of encouragement and cheer. I'm of the philosophy that kindness is often a lost art. We all live in such a hurried, complicated, high-tech world; it's easy to lose the ability to be generous or appreciative, and it's difficult to take time to be thoughtful. Toasts and tributes are a wonderful little way to slow down and give back to others words of gratitude for what they've given us. Peggy Noonan says, "Focus on a person or persons and try to see them with your kindest, most generous eyes. We are all of us flawed, but we all have brilliant gifts."[2] If it's good enough for King David in the book of Psalms, we might have something to learn from it.

Or even better, what about these words from the apostle Paul in Romans 12:10: "Love one another with

mutual affection; outdo one another in showing honor"
(NRSV). And how do you show honor? How about putting
it into words?

Are You Happy?

MARILYN MEBERG

D id you know we are living in the middle of a "happiness movement"? Major publishing houses report that in 2008 there were four thousand books written on happiness. That topic only generated fifty books in 2000. Also, increasing numbers of neuroscience studies are being done to discover new clues as to what makes us happy and what happy looks like in the brain. Enterprising self-help gurus are giving seminars assuring people of ways to achieve happiness and begin leading more fulfilling lives.

But the happiness quest has stirred up voices of opposition in the mental health professions as well. They caution we must experience unhappiness in order to feel and express healthy sorrow, natural disappointment, and loss. Those human emotions are as important to feel as happiness. Without them, people live in mindless denial and are recognizable by their use of yellow smiley faces sticking tenaciously to their foreheads.

I certainly agree we need to experience our unhappy moments and not live in denial of those events in life that hurt us. I once read a funny story about a woman who cleverly avoided an unhappy moment. She had no intention of living in denial about her real feelings. Here's her story.

Jennifer's wedding day was fast approaching, and nothing could dampen her excitement—not even her parents' nasty divorce. Her mother had found the *perfect* dress to wear and would surely be the best-dressed mother-of-the-bride ever! A week later, Jennifer was horrified to learn that her father's new, young wife had bought the exact same dress as her mother! Jennifer asked her father's new, young wife to exchange it, but she refused. "Absolutely not! I look like a million bucks in this dress, and I'm wearing it," she flatly replied.

So Jennifer told her mother, who graciously said, "Never mind, sweetheart. I'll get another dress. After all, it's your special day."

A few days later, they went shopping and did find another gorgeous dress for her mother to wear. When they stopped for lunch, Jennifer asked her mother, "Aren't you going to return the other dress? You really don't have another occasion where you could wear it."

Her mother just smiled and replied, "Of course I do, dear. I'm wearing it to the rehearsal dinner the night before the wedding."

Now of course we know the response of "I won't get mad, I'll just get even" is not a positive way of dealing with unhappy experiences. Vengeful behaviors can be as toxic as those experiences that robbed us of happiness in the first place. That being said, why all the attention to the topic of happiness, and will Jennifer's mother ever find some? Will any of us? I'd like to throw a few suggestions about how to be happy into the already existing pile of data on the subject.

There is much we can know about what does not make us happy. Perhaps we need to first take a look at some typical faulty thinking that trails along beside us on the journey to "happy." One major faulty-think is that money buys happiness. There's just enough truth to that thinking to suggest money and happiness may sleep together. The reality is, to the degree that money enables us to live comfortably, it can make us happy. For the starving and homeless people in the world, access to money can change their circumstances. It was the generous giving of money that changed Peter's life in Rwanda. Because of money, he and his family all received educations, enabling each of them to have jobs and to become self-sufficient. Those were happy-producing helps. But once our basic needs are met, money does not create happiness. The greatest faulty-think ever perpetrated upon humanity is the lie Satan tossed out to Eve. It was the lie—and she fell for it—that more is better. When we have money, the striving for more may become a driving force that can lead to unhappiness. As H. L. Mencken said, "The chief value of money lies in the fact that one lives in a world in which it is overestimated."

But we can fix the faulty thinking from the money-buys-happiness assumption by simply realizing that using money for God's purposes *does* bring happiness. So what are God's purposes? Proverbs 19:17 says, "If you help the poor, you are lending to the Lord—and he will repay you" (NLT). I suggest that one way God repays us is to provide happiness as a reward for our giving. Luke 6:38 states, "If you give, you will receive. Your gift will return to you in full measure" (NLT). Giving back to God brings us a deep level of joy and happiness.

Another faulty-think traveling along beside us on the journey to "happy" is the assumption that more leisure time would produce happiness. There is no doubt that many of us lead full lives with barely enough time to get it all done in our twenty-four-hour cycle. But apparently leisure time can be overrated. I was fascinated to read a study focused on lottery winners and how they dealt with receiving sudden wealth without working for it. The researchers compared twenty-two lottery winners to twenty-two non-lottery persons. The study revealed that, after a temporary rush of jubilation, the lottery winners were no happier than the average group of people still slugging away at their jobs. Also, the lottery people had lost much of the joy that comes from small pleasures like grabbing a cup of coffee on the way to work and listening to the morning news on the car radio. In the final analysis, researchers determined that leisure is a state of mind, which has nothing to do with what we *do* but everything to do with what we *think* and *believe.*

Although there are times when dashing off to yet another airport is an unattractive prospect, I cannot imagine my days of only sitting in a chair drinking tea and reading a book. Tea and books are my great friends, but the greatest jubilation I experience in life is knowing that I am doing what I have been called to do: communicate God's love to people who "don't get it." And when they "get it," I'm over the moon. I am truly happy.

We don't find happiness in this life without knowing

the purpose for our lives. Purpose gives us meaning, direction, and value; without purpose we drift aimlessly. One of the characters in Dostoevsky's novel *The Brothers Karamazov* stated that if a person does not live for something specific one cannot fully embrace life and would then rather destroy himself than remain on earth. I don't think Dostoevsky was talking about suicide, which destroys the human body, but about a lack of purpose, which can destroy the human soul. That's strong language, but I also believe it to be true.

There is not a human being on the planet who does not feel the immense need to know why he or she exists. Our questing for purpose, as well as happiness, is answered for us when Jesus said: "'You must love the Lord your God with all your heart, all your soul, and all your mind.' This is the first and greatest commandment. A second is equally important: 'Love your neighbor as yourself'" (Matthew 22:37–39 NLT).

What does loving God with all my heart, soul, and mind mean? It means that when Jesus extends the call to me to follow him, I do just that. I follow him to the place where my salvation is made possible—the cross. There he died for my sin. I receive his gift of salvation and then follow him in not only returning his love given for me through salvation, but then communicating that love to others. Sometimes that is no farther than my neighborhood. Sometimes it is in another country. Wherever I take the message of Jesus, that following of Jesus becomes my purpose. That following provides my happiness.

Sometimes I have missed many happy moments simply by not living out the second, equally important purpose for which I am born—loving my neighbor as myself. As a believer in Christ, I must love those "others" whom I see and those "others" about whom I know but don't see. As I have become increasingly aware of the inexplicable needs of those persons around the world living in poverty, and without access to clean water, education, or medical care, my sense of purpose broadens and becomes more clearly defined. I must and I can do something. Ephesians 2:10 says, "For we are God's workmanship, created in Christ Jesus to do good works, which God prepared in advance for us to do" (NIV). Knowing as well as believing my purpose in life is to do those "good works" God has planned for me gives me great happiness. I can't do everything, but I can do something and that something has been "prepared in advance for me to do."

So what do we say to the "happiness movement" that has spawned thousands of books hoping to point us in the direction of an achievable happiness goal? We can say happiness is not found in revenge, money, leisure, or other worldly offerings. It's found in a person named Jesus. His book spans thousands of years, documenting humanity's rebellious questing for what feels good and costs little. The bottom-line truth is this: happiness comes in giving ourselves away for a message worth a fortune.

> *You must help the weak and remember the words of the Lord Jesus, that He Himself said, "It is more blessed to give than to receive."*
>
> — ACTS 20:35 NASB

He Knows My Name

MARY GRAHAM

Get this: there is a dry cleaner in my neighborhood that I rarely frequent. In fact, I have maybe been there a dozen times total. I use another dry cleaner regularly, but on occasion I need a drop-off and pick-up in short order, so I take something on the way to work and pick it up on the way home. I did that today. Here's the amazing thing: the guy knows my name! He never does any kind of paperwork or asks me anything. He just says, with a bit of an accent, as I hand my dirty laundry through the window, "Thank you, Ms. Graham." And, although I'm rarely speechless, I just stare at him without saying anything.

As I drive away, for at least five minutes I'm thinking, *He knows my name. How in the world does he know my name?* For the life of me I cannot figure it out. We've never shared a sentence of conversation. I don't wear a name tag; I've always only paid cash for the service. I have absolutely no idea if he owns the place or manages it. I know one thing about him: he knows my name. Hmmm.

My favorite shopping mall in Dallas is far enough away that I rarely have a chance to actually shop there. When I do, I grab my bag and usually a friend or two and head straight to that mall. I always park in the same place at this particular mall, because by parking there, I can make a beeline through the makeup department, which is located in the basement of a very nice department store, famous in Dallas. I don't always stop in that store, but I always use it as a thoroughfare to the mall. It's a perfect plan. (As I say to Luci, "I know my malls.") I'm so convinced this is the best way to optimize your shopping time that I've taught all my friends to park there and use this one particular entrance for access.

One day, two or three years ago, I was racing through the makeup department to exit into the mall when I heard someone say, "Mary. Is that you? Is it you? Mary? Is it really you?" Unaccustomed as I am to being recognized, and knowing about two hundred thousand women in any given mall on any given day might be named Mary, I turned ever so slightly to the woman asking the question.

She looked at me and said, "It's you. It's you. It's really, truly you."

So I stopped. I was stunned and began to wonder if and/or how I happened to know her. She immediately put me at ease. As it turns out, her name was Sunny, and she is a group leader for Women of Faith in Dallas. She brings a group of twenty-five to a hundred women (her group keeps getting larger and larger every year) to our event at the American Airlines Center each year. But we'd never met and she had not, in fact, ever met any of the speakers personally. (Although I've taught them all my little secret about getting into that mall! And now they've all met, love, and go visit Sunny.)

We spent about an hour together while she told me story after story of absolute miracles God has done in the lives of her friends, family members, and coworkers as a result of bringing them to the Women of Faith conferences. Since that day, we've become good friends and, whenever anyone with Women of Faith flies into Dallas for any reason, I take them to meet her. (Finding that close parking lot by her store is completely incidental now—I go there for another reason!)

As I left her that first day, having visited with her for a while and also meeting some of her friends who'd been to the Women of Faith conference, I was inspired and overwhelmed with gratitude. And I was thinking, "She knows my name."

Maybe that means so much to me because of my background. My parents had eight children, and I was the eighth. When my mother needed me or wanted me to come to her, I'd hear her say, "Barbara Jan, John, Phil, *Mary*." At the sound of "Mary," I'd head toward her. I suspected she was actually calling me all along, but I could never be sure. If yours was the final name she called, it was you she was summoning. When my brothers and sisters started having their own children, all sixteen of them, for some unknown reason, called me Mimi. Now twenty-one great-nieces and -nephews call me Mimi. Even some of the children of my friends call me Mimi. When the little ones first called me by name, they had me in the palm of their baby hands. Even today, hearing those fully grown-up men and women, or the babies they've had, say, "Mimi" sends me running in their direction for any, or no, reason. And I'm the only Mimi I know, which is nice for a change.

Dale Carnegie, famous for teaching about how to win friends and influence people, said, "We should be aware of the magic contained in a person's name and realize that this single item is wholly and completely owned by the person with whom we are dealing . . . and nobody else. The name sets the individual apart; it makes him or her unique among all others. The information we are imparting or the quest we are making takes on a special importance when we approach the situation with the name of the individual. From the waitress to the senior executive, the name will work magic as we deal with others."

I see this principle in the life and ministry of Jesus. This story is told in Luke 19:1–6 of a time when Jesus called someone by name. I love this story for that reason.

> [Jesus] entered Jericho and was passing through. And there was a man called by the name of Zaccheus; he was a chief tax collector and he was rich. Zaccheus was trying to see who Jesus was, and he was unable because of the crowd, for he was small in stature. So he ran on ahead and climbed up into a sycamore tree in order to see Him, for He was about to pass through that way. When Jesus came to the place, he looked up and said to him, "Zaccheus, hurry and come down, for today I must stay at your house." And he hurried and came down and received Him gladly. (NASB)

Imagine! Jesus was a stranger to Zaccheus. Zaccheus had heard of Jesus, but never seen Him. But Zaccheus was no stranger to the Savior. Jesus called this little, short, unpopular tax collector by his name from the outset. And not only that, Jesus was ready to go to this little stranger's house. And why not? He knew him by name.

There's just something about someone calling you by your name, even when your name is as common as Mary. I don't know why exactly. It's a mystery. I guess we feel known, acknowledged, seen. Here's what's more amazing, though. Imagine this: God, the God of the universe, the God of heaven and earth, the Almighty, awesome, amazing God knows me. Furthermore, He knows my name. He's numbered the hairs on my head (for whatever reason!). He created me and knows everything there is to know about me. He sees me, calls me by name, and loves me. And He knows you, and He calls you by name, and no paperwork is required. By His spirit and through the majesty of His grace, you are His. We are His people and the sheep of His pasture. "I am the good shepherd, and I know My own and My own know Me" (John 10:14 NASB).

If I stand amazed that a total stranger remembers my name, how much more delighted and amazed can I be, knowing the One who loves me most knows me best? And if He knows me, and calls me His own, I can be sure He cares about what happens to me.

Father, thank you so much that you know us, each and every one. We are fearfully and wonderfully made. You created us uniquely and you know us intimately, as you long for us to know you. There is no one just like me nor will there ever be. And you know us by name. Your word says that you say to all who've come to know you, "You are mine. You are fearfully and wonderfully made." You call us to yourself as your dear children. Thank you that we belong to you. I pray you will give us confidence as we walk with you knowing that you created us. You know us. You care about everything that concerns us. We are yours. Your Word says, "It is You who has made us and not we ourselves." Father, thank you that you call us your children, and you call us by name.

12

Falling in Public

NICOLE C. MULLEN

For as long as I can remember, I have been an Amy Grant fan. I used to sing "Father's Eyes" into my hairbrush and pretend that I was her—well, the "brown" her. I also sang her songs as part of my morning worship. There I was as a young girl, standing beneath the predawn sky, waiting for the city bus to take my sisters and me to school. It was by the lantern pole that I would quietly sing to God and remind him that I was his girl. Years passed and my singing continued. The lantern pole and the hairbrush became stages and microphones. I learned that a life that worships Christ is still a life that will face hardship and woes, but a life that worships Christ will never face them alone. And although standing is the desired position, falling, too, has much to teach us. Because before honor comes humility.

Years later, during one of the hardest seasons of my life, I was at the end of a very bitter relationship, and was feeling as if God, too, was disappointed in me. But just when I had convinced myself that God had most likely written me off his list, I received a phone call from Amy Grant's manager saying that I had gotten the job as one her background singers. I couldn't believe it! Not because of who I would be singing with (as wonderful as she is), but because God was reminding me that he still loved me so much, and was giving me a grace gift. It was enough to undo me. It said to me that he remembered the girl who used to sing to him at the bus stop across the street from my house. He could still see her and she was loved by him. And as if it were a whisper into my heart, I heard, "I'm not mad at you!"

I spent the next year and a half with a new set of friends who felt like family, doing a one-hundred-city tour around the world. I was able to sing, dance, act crazy, and choreograph moves we did on stage. I loved every moment of it. Well, almost . . .

One night, toward the end of the U.S. portion of the tour, I must have been feeling rather confident. At this point, we had performed the same set many times in concert, and we pretty much had it down to a science. It had been a great season of learning, growth, and healing for me. I was feeling a lot stronger and a little more independent. So far, the night had gone as planned. The concert was almost over. The music began to play the hit number from the new CD we were touring, which was the background singers' cue to enter. We ran to the front of the stage and began to dance the choreographed piece we had done so many times. We began pumping our arms, lifting our feet, and enjoying the applause of the more than ten thousand people watching. And then it happened.

As if all else stood still, I began to move in slow motion. It felt like someone pulled the rug from beneath my feet. I saw myself move from the vertical into the horizontal. And within a split second I fell. Literally, I hit the floor. I was instantly faced with the dilemma of *What do I do now?* Within a split second I had to make a choice. Option A: I could start spinning in the floor and act as if I were break dancing, trying to work it into the routine; Option B: I could act as if I were really hurt, become a drama queen, garner public sympathy, and let them carry me out; or Option C: I could take a huge bite of humble pie, chew it, get back up on my feet, and continue the dance. So before my pride (which had me on the floor in the first place) could get the best of me, I went with Option C, humbled myself, and jumped right back up and into the dance.

After that encounter with the floor, I have never approached the stage, or life as a matter of fact, the same way again. I am often reminded of the scripture that says when we humble ourselves, God will exalt us, but if we exalt ourselves, he will humble us. It is a constant reminder that on the bad days I need him, and on the good days I need him. I have been called to walk the balance of keeping a good name and making myself of no reputation. Keeping my head down, but then lifting my eyes up. Standing strong and straight, yet bowing prostrate and low. It reaffirms that all foundations (except for Christ) are unstable, no matter how much fun you might be having on the stage of life. All confidence, outside of him, is simply cockiness.

The Bible tells the story of a guy named Uzzah. His household was in charge of hosting the ark of the covenant, which the Israelites believed housed the presence of God. It was sacred, it was holy, and it was very dangerous. In 1 Samuel 4, we read how Israel was fighting in battle against the Philistines and were being defeated. So the elders, without consulting the Lord, thought that they would do what had worked for Israel before. The ark of the covenant was brought up from Shiloh, and when the people saw it, their courage was renewed. The Bible says that they shouted so loudly the earth shook. When the enemy heard this, and understood that the presence of the

Israelites' God had come into the camp, they were terri-fied. In 1 Samuel 4:7–8, the Philistines said, "God has come into the camp! . . . Woe to us! For such a thing has never happened before. Woe to us! Who will deliver us . . . These are the gods who struck the Egyptians with all the plagues in the wilderness" (NKJV).

But, since Israel did not ask God for direction and brought the ark out without his blessing, they were defeated. The ark was taken by the enemy. Once it was in Philistine territory, it was placed in the temple of their god Dagon. When the people came to worship the next morning, they found Dagon, their idol, fallen in the dirt, on its face before this ark (as if in worship). So they set it back up. The next morning, the same thing happened again except this time the head and hands had fallen off, and only the torso remained. Eventually the people of the land became spooked because wherever they would take the ark, the people in that place would develop tumors, and many died. The Philistines cried out, "'They have brought the ark of the God of Israel to us to kill us and our people!' So they sent and gathered together all the lords of the Philistines, and said, 'Send away the ark of the God of Israel, and let it go back to its own place'" (1 Samuel 5:10–11 NKJV). And so they returned it to Israel, with guilt offer-ings in tow.

When the ark was finally returned to the Israelites, they let their curiosity get the best of them and they looked into the ark, which was strictly forbidden. According to the American Standard Version of the Bible (Hebrew to English translation) and the Septuagint (Hebrew to Greek), God slew 50,070 men because of this action. Many years later, during King David's rule, he called for the ark to be brought up to Jerusalem. There was music and much celebration until Uzzah, one of the sons of Abinadab, reached out and touched the ark. For this irreverent act, God struck him dead. Uzzah's—and Israel's—mistake was in forgetting the ultimate reverence they were to show God.

Because Uzzah's family had housed the ark for many years, he must have been familiar with the stories of what the ark of the covenant had done to the Philistines and to the idol Dagon, as well as to the fifty thousand plus Israelites who had died. Still, perhaps he took it for granted and thought, *It could never happen to me.*

I am glad that God, in his mercy, allowed my fall onstage that night to be embarrassing and not fatal. That fall helped me to remember that I'm human, and I am capable of making mistakes—*big* mistakes. It also reminded me of the gift of God's grace and mercy to me. I know that I am invited to come to his throne boldly, but I am also commanded to approach him humbly. God alone has set the boundaries of the earth; He alone is the inventor of life. There is none like Him in intellect, in power, in love. And no one else is worthy of our falling face down in worship, day after day, time and time again.

13

Sparks

PATSY CLAIRMONT

Pretend you are doing something that you haven't done before that you'd love to try. What might that look like? Would you be in the corporate world? Or a pilot perhaps? A stylist? A café owner . . . say, in Tuscany? Perhaps you'd be retired? Swinging in a hammock sipping strawberry lemonade in Barbados? Or are you a risk taker? Scaling a mountain? Bobbing in a hot air balloon over Africa? Or running a day care center? (That takes moxie!) Perchance you'd be a concert pianist, a celebrated orator, or an award-winning poet?

Still no ideas? Well, let's try this, answer the age-old question, "When I grow up what do I want to be?" Emphasis on "want."

Here, I'll start; I want to be a novelist . . . an artist . . . a photographer . . . and for sure a home decorator. Oh, and I want to be a gift shop owner. One where accessories abound and encouragement is the hallmark of the store. Ah, yes, and a master gardener, capable of maintaining a menagerie of plants and a profuse tangle of flowers. Please add to my list owner of a home magazine. I'd call it, "Short Stuff . . . quick ideas for dynamic living." I'd like to be a chef, but then I found out I'd actually have to cook, so, never mind. I just really like the way people's faces light up when you say "chef." (My idea of gourmet cooking is oatmeal, deviled eggs, and fried potatoes. Those are my current specialties along with popcorn and tall drafts of icy water. Actually, if I do say so myself, I rather excel at the last one.)

Truth be told I don't have that much time, energy, or even motivation left to pursue all those desirable occupations. I've already used up a truckload of calendars in this life. I think somebody must have put them on speed dial when I wasn't looking, so at this seasoned stage of my journey it's more fun for me, when I'm not speaking, writing, and traveling, to just to think out of the box of the myriad of possibilities.

Do you ever wonder why God gave us the capacity to think over the top? He certainly colors way outside the lines. We see that in starlit nights, rainbows, the Milky

Way. Do you think when He designed us after His own image, including the capacity for imagining, it was meant to be used just to entertain ourselves during recess? Or fill-up hours in old age? No way.

Personally I think it would be terribly boring and depressing if we could not move beyond what we know or are experiencing right now. Don't you? I think imagination adds to inspiration, to keep vitality in our dreams, which in turn oxygenates us. In other words, I think our over-the-top thinking has the potential to be life-bearing.

In this age of polluted water, cockeyed weather, stock crashes, food-chain dilemmas, and horrific violence I could use a big dose of "life-bearing." So many aspects of life are tainted. Now don't get me wrong. I'm not suggesting we sit around and sulk, wishing for what we don't have. Why that has all the markings of an ingrate. We don't want that. But to divinely think outside ourselves is to willingly open the door of our limitations to find a path to higher ground. If we think about it, we've seen that in the inspired lives of many who have gone before us.

As a kid growing up in Michigan, when our family had out-of-town visitors, it meant we would soon be on our way to Greenfield Village, for a day of adventure. The Village is a historical site that depicts the life and career of Henry Ford and other greats, like his good friend Thomas

Edison. Maybe it was the early introduction to Edison's life or the gratitude I felt for his invention of the phonograph, so as a teen I could be-bop around my bedroom in time to "Blue Suede Shoes," but he has always been a favorite famous figure of mine. Not as much as Elvis, but still on my top who's who list. Actually Thomas Edison is a notable to many. *Life* magazine in 1997 listed him as number one of "The 100 Most Important People in the Past 1000 Years." Wow! That's saying something. More recently in 2005 he was voted by the public as number fifteen on the Greatest Americans television series. Oops, Thomas slipped a little, but still an impressive showing.

Who knew two filaments setting off a spark would generate such lasting enthusiasm? And while the invention of the commercial incandescent lightbulb might be one of his greatest, it certainly wasn't his only one. Edison held 1,093 patents in the U.S. alone.

And get this, he had a whopping total of three months of formal education. His elementary teacher said Thomas's brain was addled. Just think, under what appeared to be a confused child's thoughts, lay all the seeds of a genius. Addled? Futuristic would be more like it, why the man was a visionary. I wonder how many times that instructor ate those words through Edison's mentally fertile career. Thomas was a man who thought beyond what he knew, always asking the question "what if" and then vigorously pursuing dreams. In fact, Edison is credited with the first industrial research laboratory. This over-the-top man was so ahead of his time he already saw the potential of think tanks.

Over Edison's desk hung the sign, the quote, "There is no expedient to which a man will not resort to avoid the real labor of thinking." And while that appears to be a round about way to say, use your mind, use your imagination, Thomas's life was a direct and steady path of doing just that. In spite of his deafness, the death of his first wife, business controversy, and his struggle with diabetes, Edison remained creative until his last breath, which, by the way, his son captured in a test tube and sealed. Strange? Yep. But somehow consistent with a man who believed we were just one test tube away from another life-changing invention. He also had a plaster death mask made . . . too bad it wasn't a brain mask, I would have liked to borrow that.

I love people who are inspired. They fan a flame in me. They remind me to think outside the box. I was better at that as a child, and even a teen, but my creative thoughts were snuffed out as a young adult when I found myself boxed in by agoraphobia. Becoming a prisoner of one's home stifles hope and causes one to become myopic. I only saw doom and gloom, and my imaginings were frightening, the kind we are warned to cast down.

It took me years of growing healthy in Christ to refind good mental health. I learned there is a difference between vain imaginations, which are self-centered and destructive and can be fueled by fear, and inspired thoughts, those that are centered on Christ and His elevated principles for our lives. Left to my own tendencies, my mind can become quickly corrupt, but protected and guided by God's Spirit I can move to a higher quality of existence.

Recently my husband of forty-seven years and I were having a spat-filled season. We both seemed to have a "case of cranky" toward the other. As a marriage veteran, may I just say this is not unusual with mates to go through ups and downs, some unexplainable. It's a feature in the cycle of relationships, whether it's mates, friends, or relatives. As humans we can't totally avoid our insecure, judgmental, oversensitive human responses. They crop up like weeds. Ah, but we don't have to let them flourish.

Then one day I had an epiphany about the way I was hearing Les, so I changed my approach, and I began praying-attention: not just listening to Les, but praying as I listened. This caused me to hear him differently. I was thinking our friction was just his fault, but as I prayed-attention, I realized I was adding a lot of unnecessary sparks to our contention.

When I opened my mind, which is one of the benefits of a challenged mind, the fresh breeze of possibility wafted through; in this case, the possibility that I was an active participant in the dissension. Because of that insight I was willing to think differently about my behavior, to think what I might do that could temper my own responses, which led me to the breakthrough thought to not just pay attention, but to pray-attention. It was like I needed a divine filter on my perceptions to see my own behavior more clearly.

Are you stuck in a bad cycle of interaction, a sad cycle of self-pity, or a mad cycle of judgment? I suggest you try opening your mind, even a centimeter, and then ask God to give you creative solutions, different from anything you have tried. Sometimes we run out of bright ideas and settle into shadowed ruts, but God never runs out of dazzling ideas. Talk about a think tank, He's the originator. He's more than two filaments sparking, Christ is the light of the world. He's not an inventor, He is our Creator. And an over-the-top one at that . . . just look around.

14

Highs and Lows

〰 SANDI PATTY

In the fall of 2008, Don and I had a wonderful experience in the beautiful mountains of North Carolina. Every year our pastor hosts a three-day event at The Cove, which is run by the Billy Graham Foundation. It is such a beautiful setting in which to have Bible studies, devotions, sing-alongs, quiet times, together times. I was the musical guest and did a concert, but the rest of the time we got to totally relax. They let Don and me have one of the gorgeous cabins on the property, and my parents got to attend as well. It was a great time for Don and me to be together and to be with my parents.

But if I can be perfectly honest, I didn't even want to go. I was tired; I had been traveling so much. I was pouty and I just wanted to stay home. But Don and I hadn't had a "date" in a long time and so I threw some things in my suitcase and off we went, bad attitude and all. It wasn't pretty.

We stayed in a lovely cabin on top of the mountain, and it was stocked with some light snacks and drinks. Don played golf during the day and I relaxed and went for walks. One day, feeling ambitious, I decided to walk *up* the mountain. Of course thinking that was a good idea—yeah, right! I began to walk up, up, up. Thankfully, it wasn't straight up all the time. It would level out for a bit, and then I'd head up, up, up again. It was a great workout, and there were thoughtful places along the path where one could sit for a bit and see the most beautiful views. And the higher I got, the more beauty there was to see.

The path ended, and I decided to stay at the top for a few moments and absorb the incredible scenery. From way up there at the top, I could clearly see the whole valley, and it was easy to see the plan for the valley—the roads and paths were clearly laid out. From up there I was able to appreciate the valley and its beauty. From up there, the valley made sense.

In our own lives, we often long for the mountaintop experience and dread our times in the valley. Why is it that, in the daily-ness of life, it is hard to appreciate the valley? When you're down there, it's confusing. It doesn't make sense, and there are times it's downright scary. But there can be beauty in the valley if we just see it from the right perspective:

> Not only so, but we also rejoice in our sufferings, because we know that suffering produces perseverance; perseverance, character; and character, hope. And hope does not disappoint us, because God has poured out his love into our hearts by the Holy Spirit, whom he has given us. (Romans 5:3–5 NIV)

Trials and perseverance bring hope? I love that!

You know, when I was walking up that mountain, there was nothing else for me to do but put one foot in front of the other—to persevere. There wasn't a whole lot of hope in those steps, but those steps led me to hope. And so, in a way, the hope is what kept me going. And the mountaintop was glorious. It helped me be thankful—yes, thankful—for the valleys. I prayed up on top of the mountain that day that, the next time I found myself in a valley in my life, I would stop and be thankful and that I wouldn't forget how beautiful the valley times can be.

I also realized that it took me a whole lot longer to get *up* the mountain than it took me to get *down* into the valley. How true of life as well. So I am learning never to take the mountaintops for granted, for they only last for a season. And then another valley comes, but it only lasts for a season as well. And *through it all* (hey, that sounds like a song I know!), God is faithful.

Part 3

15

Marking the Turf

✎ NICOLE C. MULLEN

We live out in the country, and so we have always had "outside" dogs. On two different occasions we have had two different dogs with the same name—JD (aka "Jasmine's dog"). When my daughter Jasmine was about three years old, we welcomed a medium-sized, black, good-natured, "summa" dog into our family. We always joked that *summa* stood for "some of this, some of that" because his pedigree was a mystery. JD was loyal, but he had a passion for chasing cars. After about five years, his passion proved to be fatal. It happened a few days before Jasmine's eighth birthday. She had been asking for another dog for the occasion, and her father was strongly considering it, but when my nephew notified me that JD was lying in the front yard, unmoving, my husband's strong maybe turned into a quick, definite yes. So, quietly and unbeknownst to our firstborn daughter, the search began.

Somewhere along the border of Alabama, in a litter of stronger canines, we chose the smallest and the weakest. He was grey, a little awkward, and very cute. He was a Weimaraner. He was concealed until the night of the birthday slumber party, and he was a big hit with Jasmine and her friends. When someone asked what his name was, David and I piped in and said, "JD!" Our daughter immediately accepted the title, probably thinking, *OK, I guess now I'll just have two JDs.* In a somber tone, without hysteria, we announced that the original JD had been hit by a car, and now she had another JD to love. She paused for a second, out of respect for the only dog she had loved, and then as if she digested the bitter pill of saying good-bye, quickly moved on. She would never forget her first dog, never stop loving him, but she still had more love on the inside to give to this new little pup.

When the second JD was about a year old, Josiah, our youngest, was born. JD, who was sweet and a bit on the clumsy side, took an instant liking to our son. But Josiah didn't always see it that way. When you are learning to walk, you begin to see life from a higher vantage point than when you were crawling around on the floor, and you begin to feel like a big kid. But the moment an animal, whose head stands just a bit taller than yours, starts running toward you (even if it is a happy run), the natural tendency of a child (and some grown-ups too) is to run away in the opposite direction. This was Josiah's reaction. He was always OK when he was stroking JD's head from the safety of my arms, but the moment he was to stand on his own, face-to-face with the same creature, fear made his little legs move and an extra dose of courage was needed.

On more than one occasion I immediately lowered myself to the same level, stood with him, and showed him how to stroke JD's head. I told Josiah/JD that he was a good dog, and gave him the power to say, "No, JD" when the dog tried to jump on him or he sensed that JD was being naughty. Josiah liked his new authority. JD didn't seem to care and must have thought that my son was funny. He never took offense at this toddler who was constantly trying to boss him around.

By the next year, we had a total of four dogs. But JD considered himself Josiah's chief protector. Whenever Josiah and a friend would stand on the slats of the wooden fence out back and invite the horses to come near, JD would have to be the first dog to come to Josiah's rescue to chase the horses away. And of course Josiah would yell,

"No, JD!" But the dog would just smile with his mouth wide open as if to say, "I'll keep you safe. Aren't you proud of me?"

One morning, during the days when Jasmine and I would take daily walks, Josiah came along for the ride in his stroller. Because we live in the country, the dogs (at this time all four of them) came along too. We would often walk past one house in the neighborhood that had several dogs behind its fence. As we got closer to the house, all of the dogs began barking at each other. This particular day I scolded my dogs and called them back. JD was determined not to leave Josiah's side, and suddenly, while keeping his eyes on the fenced-in dogs, he moved a little closer to Josiah, raised his back leg and peed on Josiah's shin. I couldn't believe it! This dog actually peed on my baby.

"No, JD!" was all I could say at that moment. What I was really thinking was, *OK, I knew you were a little bit off, but now you must have lost it! Did my baby really look like a tree to you?!* JD just looked at us, mouth wide open and smiling as if to say, "I'll keep you safe. Aren't you proud of me?" I didn't want to hurt his feelings, but I was tempted. Before I could speak my mind, my neighbor came out of his house with paper towels in hand. He had witnessed the exchange and wanted to help me clean up the mess. "Can you believe JD would pee on my baby?" I said.

My neighbor chuckled and said, "You really *do* have a good dog. He was just being protective, telling the other dogs that your baby belongs to him. He was marking his turf, and was vowing to defend it."

Instantly, I felt like a heel and started stroking his head saying, "Good dog, good dog!" over and over again. I felt embarrassed that I had misunderstood his actions, as unusual as they were. But I could tell that he had already forgiven me.

In a much, ahem, *grander* fashion, the Bible teaches in Psalm 34:7 that "the angel of the LORD encamps around those who fear him, and he delivers them" (NIV). God's angels are commissioned to stand guard over us that fear and respect God. They have marked the turf around us with strength and valor. They fight forces both seen and unseen to deliver us from danger. Scripture also states that "he who dwells in the shelter of the Most High will rest in the shadow of the Almighty. . . . For he will command his angels concerning you to guard you in all your ways . . . 'Because he loves me,' says the LORD, 'I will rescue him; I will protect him, for he acknowledges my name'" (Psalm 91:1, 11, 14 NIV).

God ultimately owns our times and seasons, our places and events. He has created us for what we will need on the journey of life and has mapped out our route. His splendor awaits us at the final destination. It is for the in-between times that we are in need of his protection, guarding and guiding us. Until that day, when his purpose has been completed in us, we can be thrilled and content. For his outstretched arm can reach us, his all-seeing eyes will keep us, his everlasting love will be upon us, and because of him, we are safe.

16

The Upside of Failure

MARILYN MEBERG

Last week I was having one of those in-depth conversations with my grandson Alec that may stick in my mind forever. We were discussing the character "Tony" in the hit TV series 24 and were trying to determine if Tony really is a bad guy or one who is going to surprise us at the end of the series and become a good guy after all. Alec, a bright kid who is in the gifted program at school, told me, in a lowered voice meant only for my ears, that Tony is going to stay bad. He said Tony tricked us in the beginning of the series into thinking he would be a good guy, loyal to Jack Bauer and the fight to keep America safe from terrorists, but that was never "his passion." "His passion," Alec told me, "is to destroy America."

That was a sobering bit of prophecy for me because I always liked Tony and hated thinking he would act out his destructive passions on America. Wanting to get deeper into Alec's appraisal of Tony's character, I asked Alec to tell me why Tony went bad in the first place.

"Well, Maungya, Tony is suffering from an accumulation of failures that make him angry and bitter."

I dropped my fork. "Alec Soule, you are only twelve years old. Where did you learn that shrink talk and how do you know how to toss the word 'accumulation' into that sentence?"

He patiently responded by saying, "You know I'm in the gifted program, Maungya; that's just gifted talk."

I had to stuff my napkin in my mouth to cover up my gleeful reaction. There's no doubt that kid is gifted and certainly no doubt he is adorable.

But I wasn't finished probing his mind about Tony's "accumulation of failures" and how they had caused him to become angry and bitter. So later I questioned Alec about Tony's "stuff" and his response to his stuff, and why Alec assumed the accumulation of failures led to an angry, bitter spirit. Again, in that patient voice Alec uses with me, which makes me wonder if he thinks I'm dumb, old, or both, he said, "Failures hurt very deeply Maungya. That's just how it works!"

That comment pained my heart—I was sure it had a personal root. I wondered if I had the right to reach into the

depths of his little boy heart and hear about his own per-
ceived failures.

The next day he and I were playing "Horse." I can't possibly explain that game except to say it requires a basketball
and a hoop. Alec is a very good basketball player. I was too
at one time, but of course it was 246 years ago. It pleased me
that my one-handed shot still had a fairly good rate of accu-
racy. It pleased me also to have Alec occasionally say, "Hey,
good shot Maungya." I modestly acted as if I was surprised
each time the ball wobbled through the net. That strategy
would keep him thinking my good shots would be infre-
quent and he might become careless. That would mean
he'd get the letters *H-O-R-S-E* before I did. My win!

During a time out, called by me, I asked Alec if he had
a philosophy and if he did, what was his philosophy of
failure? It was my turn to sound patient as I explained that
a philosophy, a personal philosophy is made up of how you
think about life and how you think life operates. Your philosophy is based on your attitudes, and your attitudes
decide how you act. I totally had his attention. He let the
ball roll idly down the driveway into the rosebushes.

"You know Maungya, I don't always have a good attitude. I get really mad sometimes. When I get mad, kids
pull back from me. They think I'm a bad sport who always
has to win at everything."

"If you don't win, Alec, do think you are a failure? No one wins all the time at anything. I'm trying to beat you in horse, but if I lose, I'm not a failure. I simply didn't make as many accurate shots as you did. It's a matter of my attitude. My attitude is made up of what I think about myself and the things that happen to me. The same thing is true about you. Your attitude is simply what you think about yourself, and what happens to you every day is then interpreted by your attitude."

I guess that was getting a bit heavy, so Alec pulled the basketball from the rosebushes and said "OK, Maungya, let's see what happens to your philosophy when I win this round of horse."

He won. But that discussion of what makes up a personal philosophy, which is based on personal attitudes, which then produces behaviors, continued beyond the horse game. I was not a loser because I lost at horse anymore than he was winner because he beat me at horse. What we think about ourselves determined that. But I had to explain to him the value of having a philosophy of failure, because he will need it all his life. Otherwise, he will define himself only as a winner when he has winning experiences. Life is made up of many losing experiences—of failures. What does a person think about those failures? What is the attitude used to interpret those failures? Alec needed to think about the answers to those questions to determine his philosophy.

The next time we were together, I congratulated myself on having the forethought to save some interesting statistics about Michael Jordan I had read some time ago. Fortunately, it was tucked into a corner of my billfold for "such a time as this."

"So, OK, Alec, tell me what you think about this. Michael Jordan missed more than nine thousand shots in his career and lost three hundred games. Twenty-six times he missed the game-winning shot. Did he have a philosophy of failure? If he did, what was it?"

Being the gifted kid he is, Alec thought deeply for several minutes. Finally he said, "OK, Maungya, I get what you're saying. Jordan had to think he was a great basketball player even if he missed shots. That was his attitude about himself. And when he blew those twenty-six games and when he missed the game-winning shots, he needed a philosophy of failure." A long silence followed and then he said, "What good is a philosophy of failure? How does that help? He blew those games. I would feel horrible!"

We agreed Jordon must have felt horrible, but that was when his philosophy of failure needed to kick in. He couldn't give up and say, "I don't have what it takes to be a great basketball player . . . I've missed too many shots. Maybe basketball isn't my game." Instead he thought about ways to improve his skills, ways to get better and better. He would not give up; he would work even harder than he had ever worked before. A philosophy of failure means you don't give up even if you have some failures; you keep working.

Alec brightened up and again told me he was "getting" what I was saying. He told me about a report he had done in school about Thomas Edison, who had tried out thousands of different kinds of lightbulbs before finally inventing one that worked. "So." Alec said, "I guess he had a philosophy of failure . . . right, Maungya?" Bingo.

As I was leaving for home after those great conversations with Alec, he said, "Ya know, Maungya, Tony (from 24) needs to work on how he thinks about himself. That could change his personal philosophy. If he did that, he could become a good guy by the end of the series."

There's no doubt that kid is gifted, and also adorable.

There's a huge spiritual lesson in all this that goes far beyond adjusting our attitudes, monitoring our behavior, and having successful failure philosophies. All that "human stuff" is sound psychology, but the reassuring truth is that God has provided a foolproof failure policy for each of us. If we understand it, it will no longer be a policy or a philosophy; it will be a theology.

Those of us who are believers know about God's

failure-theology even if we have not called it that. But we tend to forget it from time to time and edge off into basic humanism, which says, "Get a grip . . . do it yourself." We *can't* do it ourselves. God does not expect us to "get a grip and do it ourselves." Why not? Because he knows we can't do it—not indefinitely. We weren't created for failure, but the crash of sin, which still reverberates from the Garden, has ensured us of failure experiences.

To be human is to make mistakes, to sometimes fail. Sometimes we fail miserably. We hate that. It robs us of self-confidence and self-esteem. If it is a public failure, we are humiliated and want to hide somewhere so as not to be seen and judged further by the criticisms of those who witnessed our failure.

So what is God's failure-theology? It is expressed simply and profoundly in Micah 7:8: "For though I fall, I will rise again" (NLT). My failures are evidence of a humanity prone to failing. I need to know that, remember that. God's promise is to pick me up that I might, in His strength, rise again . . . over and over again.

If I think in ways that don't allow for the potential of failure, I am setting myself up as one who does not need God. That thinking encourages a human self-reliance that can lead to arrogance. It could leak into a thinking of, *I need God for salvation but otherwise, I can take care of myself. I don't need to even pray about that. . . . I simply need to use common sense!*

Another dimension of God's failure-theology is that our failures give us the opportunity to see how God works everything together for good. All of our bad choices and miserable failures are perfect opportunities for us to witness his endless love and creativity. Our failures show us how perfectly God puts all our broken and fragmented pieces together again. Munch on this fantastic scripture from Colossians 1:19–20:

> So spacious is he, so roomy, that everything of God finds its proper place in him without crowding. Not only that, but all the broken and dislocated pieces of the universe—people and things, animals and atoms—get properly fixed and fit together in vibrant harmonies, all because of his death, his blood that poured down from the cross. (MSG)

What an amazing truth! If I win or lose playing horse, or anything else in life, God fits everything together again. When he lifts me up, I don't let go of his hand or think I can make it without him. He holds me and sees me through every failure. Why does he do this for me? Because he thinks I'm worth it. To him there's no doubt I'm a winner.

17

Ticked

PATSY CLAIRMONT

Pick my left pocket of its silver dime, but spare the right—it holds my golden time!

—OLIVER WENDELL HOLMES

I have just arrived home from an over-the-top vacation with my husband, Les. We were really good to ourselves and decided to take a whole week for each other. A whole week! Why that's 10,080 minutes! Of course, let me preface this by saying it had been years since we darted off without family or didn't incorporate work into a getaway . . . so I'm thinking it was about time.

It wasn't until we were in flight for our trip that I turned to Les and asked, "When is the last time we did this, just you and me?" His first answer was "never," but after mentally scouring through the years I remembered a vacation we took with friends.

We didn't mean to wait years but somehow time

slipped through the hourglass of our lives with liquid speed. It seemed like one night we climbed into bed young and the next morning we woke up qualified for senior discounts at the local coffee shop. Les and I just celebrated our forty-seven wedding anniversary, so you have to admit we've used up some serious sand in the hourglass of time.

Actually I'm considering giving up my wristwatch, which keeps losing time and going back to hourglasses. I just can't figure out how to strap it on my wrist, I'm sure I'd have sand strewn everywhere. But my watch has been in for repairs six times in six months. What's with that? A watch that can't hold its minutes isn't worth much, especially in our fast-paced, minute-motivated lifestyle.

Friends, Randy and Chris, decided to slow their existence down by hiking the winding Appalachian Trail. Randy had been on the footpath to Blood Mountain many times, but this was Chris's first time to join him. Her idea of a stroll through the woods and Randy's turned out to be very different, because once his feet hit the path, Randy's need to push quickly to the top surfaced and soon caused friction between them.

At first Chris was half-running to keep up, thinking Randy would eventually slow down and they would begin to enjoy the scenery. All the while Randy was hoping

Chris would pick up her pace and not lag behind so they could make it to the top at a respectable pace. Finally breathless and discouraged that she was trotting past the very things she had come along to enjoy, Chris filed her complaint.

"Look around at the beauty, Randy," she exclaimed. "Examine the violets. Investigate the streams. Listen to the sparrows song. Let's not miss this beauty in a wild dash to the top," Chris pleaded.

Randy heard Chris. Well, at first he had to work at shifting his will into second gear, but once Randy entered into the beauty of the moss-ladened trees, observed the South Carolina wrens flitting through tree-filtered sun rays, and took time for the wildlife views from craggy ledges, he realized that while he had been on this path before, there was much he hadn't even noticed much less enjoyed. Why? Because Randy was on a ticking race to the finish line.

Ever feel that way? Constantly aware of your need to keep moving? Like Captain Hook in Peter Pan being stalked by the alligator who had swallowed a clock, and now minutes nip at your heels.

Sometimes I wonder if it is the attaining of a goal that should be our priority or the journey toward the goal. Probably both, don't you think? It's just I can get myself into such an emotional wad darting forward in constant competition with a relentless clock that I miss things that are right along my path. I mean, I know its unrealistic to think I can manage my time so well that I won't ever be rushed. I know I can't always stop to enjoy the sparrow's melodious song or pull off on the side of the road to gather a fistful of violets. But I also don't want to arrive at the finish line empty-handed and without a song in my heart.

During our vacation, two of our friends were in the swimming pool when one turned to the other and asked, "I'm here, are you here?" The friend paused, considered the question and then replied, "Yes, I am here, are you?"

What a smart way to remind each other to show up where you're at so you don't miss the party. And it's a great question because mental boot-scootin' can keep us preoccupied to the point that we can actually drive to a destination and upon arrival not know how we got there, because we had other things on our minds. I've done that, haven't you? Scary. Or how many times have you had to ask someone to repeat what they've just said because while your body was standing in their presence your brain was counting coconuts from a hammock in Maui? Or you were mentally finishing up a project at home. Or you had already moved on to the next appointment.

Years ago as I walked into a gathering, I overheard a

pastor of a megachurch whisper to his wife, "Remember, arrive leaving." That statement rattled around in my head for a long time. His wife told me that statement was his mantra. I'm aware that was how this motivator achieved so much, but at that time I couldn't imagine the disconnect and pressure of never being fully where you're at. Now as I look back, I realize I have often done that. I just hadn't put it into words.

Staying present and staying on time seem to be constant sources of life-tension. My friend Luci is always reminding audiences, "To live the life out of every day." That's what I want to do. I want to be present in the current moment and live my life with a pocketful of confetti so I'm prepared to celebrate.

Which is what Western Europe hoped to do, as it began pulling out of the Dark Ages, when, for one thing, the first mechanical clock was invented. For years people were clueless as to the exact hour in a given day. Hmm, I wonder how they set appointments during those watchless years? "I'll meet you at Krispy Kreme for a glazed doughnut at three granules past one inch of sand"?

Actually, my husband feels I'm three granules short of an hourglass when it comes to measuring time. I confess I don't have a good sense of how fast an hour can flit by or how long five minutes takes to sweep off a clock's face. I'm afraid I have left Les sitting in the car strumming his fingers on the steering wheel more times than I dare count, while he waited for me to emerge from the house or store. I guess there's only so many times a guy can thump out "She'll Be Comin' Around the Mountain," before he begins to honk out the song, "Born to Lose."

The Scripture warns us about losing time by reminding us to redeem it. "Redeem" is a foundational word in the life of faith meaning to make an exchange.

I remember as a child shopping at the Redemption Store with my mom. She use to collect green and gold stamps that you received in those days when you bought groceries and gas. Actually I still have a few of those stray stamps floating around in boxes of old pictures; they're probably by now, like me, antique.

I helped mom paste the stamps in designated books so we could redeem them for merchandise. In fact, that's how I got my first set of luggage when I married. Mom and I sat and licked hundred of stamps until our tongues were shriveled and dry, then we exchanged those stacks of bulging books for my wedding gift. I walked out of the Redemption Store, forty-seven years ago, sporting three pieces of light blue cardboard luggage, that lasted thirty years. (They just don't make cardboard like they used to.)

What do you redeem your time for? If you could track

your minutes in a twenty-four-hour period what "merchandise" will you have gained in exchange for your time? Perhaps the building of memories with a child? Now that's what I call priceless. Or the reading of a fine novel? For me, in the bustle of my demands, that's a wise mental investment. Maybe you use up a lot of time worrying, griping, stewing, or blaming? From personal experience I can tell you those are poor swaps. Or you might have exchanged your hours dreaming an old dream that's past its expiration date? Or rehashing mistakes? Positively, not worth it.

In the book of Ecclesiastes is a time clock of sorts . . . listen to it tick:

A time to be born,
And a time to die:
A time to plant,
And a time to pluck what is planted:
A time to kill,
And a time to heal:
A time to break down,
And a time to build up.
A time to weep,
And a time to laugh:
A time to mourn,
And a time to dance:

A time to cast away stones,

And a time to gather stones:

A time to embrace,

And a time to refrain from embracing:

A time to gain,

And a time to lose:

A time to keep,

And a time to throw away:

A time to tear,

And a time to sew:

A time to keep silence,

And a time to speak:

A time to love,

And a time to hate:

A time of war,

And a time of peace.

—Ecclesiastes 3:2–8

Tick tock tick tock. While we were not meant to rush frantically through our allotted hours, we surely don't want to ignore the sands of time. Purposed living allows us to put our head on the pillow at night and rest in quietness and peace knowing we have fully participated in the gift of life.

"I'm here, are you here?"

18

Centered in Him

LUCI SWINDOLL

A few months ago I walked by my big world globe in the library and noticed the center line that goes all the way around it was falling off. *What happened?* I asked myself. But before I could answer, I took the end of it between two fingers and peeled it off completely, rolled it up, and put it in a little plastic bag. Then I wrote on the bag, *Center of the world. Don't throw this away.* I added the date and slipped it into my middle desk drawer. Since then, every time I open the drawer, there's the center of the world staring me in the face as if to say, "Don't lose me, I'm important. I hold the world together."

From that, here's where my mind goes—there've been times in the past I actually thought my world was falling apart at the seams. The center was coming unwound. I didn't know what to do about a certain dilemma or was confused as to what direction I should take. I wasn't even completely sure what I believed or what I stood for. All my uncertainties were staring me in the face. And you can be sure, if I'd had my center of the world tape in a little bag somewhere, I would've used it.

A poem by the great Irish poet W. B. Yeats addresses some of these same issues. This is the first verse from "The Second Coming":

> Turning and turning in the widening gyre
> The falcon cannot hear the falconer;
> Things fall apart; the centre cannot hold;
> Mere anarchy is loosed upon the world,
> The blood-dimmed tide is loosed, and everywhere
> The ceremony of innocence is drowned;
> The best lack all conviction, while the worst
> Are full of passionate intensity.[3]

Although this poem was written ninety years ago, its message is applicable to us today. It was written as the First World War had ended and the world had lost its center. Yeats was dismayed at the prospect of uncontrollable changes. Everything was in flux. He didn't talk about what it was exactly that bugged him, but we know Yeats had the sense that things were being ripped apart at the center, and he feared order would collapse. Valuable, cultural traditions would be left behind. I realize we've come a long way from 1920 when this poem was written, but that same sense of something big happening on the horizon is still with us. It causes us to wonder how we can prepare for the fires of imagination that might cause us to lose hope . . . or come apart at the seams.

Interestingly, the Bible has a lot to say about the center *not* coming apart. Look at these verses from *The Message*:

> God is supremely esteemed. His **center** holds. (Isaiah 33:5)

> Our firm decision is to work from this focused **center**: One man died for everyone. That puts everyone in the same boat. He included everyone in his death so that everyone could also be included in his life, a resurrection life, a far better life than people ever lived on their own. (2 Corinthians 5:15)

> It's wonderful what happens when Christ displaces worry at the **center** of your life. (Philippians 4:7)

> God holds the high **center**, he sees and sets the world's mess right. (Psalm 9:7)

If we keep these thoughts in mind, we're prepared for what comes our way. When Christ is our center it is he who enables us to maintain peace no matter how disconcerting our situation may become. As Isaiah said, "His center holds."

About forty years ago I began taking a hard look at my life, trying to determine what course of action to take regarding future plans. In so doing, I decided to write a creed that would serve as my definition, describe what I valued, and help me with decision-making for the years to come. I wanted something that would stand the test of time, that would not change from year to year. I wanted this creed to be my center. So, after thinking systematically through my beliefs, this is what I wrote:

1. I believe in Jehovah God, the God of the Bible, to Whom I have access because of my trust in the justifying death of His Son, Jesus Christ.

2. I believe God to be an entity unto Himself, a Will without conflict, the Prime Mover of history, and the Personal Guide for my life by means of His Living Word (Jesus Christ) and His Written Word (the Bible).

3. I believe that no form or degree of reformation has ever been, can now be, or will ever be an adequate or

satisfying substitute for God's plan for regeneration of the human heart, as stated in the Bible.

4. I believe regeneration to be the absolutely essential factor for humanity to know the real meaning of life, and I believe this to be the first foundation stone to abundant living.

5. I believe Jesus Christ to be the unique Person of the universe: true and complete deity with perfect and sinless humanity united in one Person forever.

6. I believe all humanity to be born depraved and without hope until each person individually puts his or her trust in Jesus Christ (and Him alone) through an act of his or her own volition, as energized by God's Spirit.

7. I believe I will receive from life in direct proportion to that part of myself I am able and willing to give.

8. I believe individuals to be of more value than things, quality of more value than happiness, forgiveness of more value than pride, sincerity of more value than artificiality, and beauty of more value than adornment.

9. I believe in creative, industrious living that finds its source in a constructive challenge.

10. I believe in the expression of understanding and knowledge by means of reading, travel, the arts, observation, experience, and the best use of solitude.

11. I believe in the right to opinions and preferences, based upon consideration of known facts as well as Spirit-guided perception.

12. I believe in the power and motivation of positive thinking, a sense of humor, self-discipline, flexible planning, consideration and acceptance of others, open-mindedness, imagination, and self-control.

13. In summary, and on the basis of the above affirmation, I express this to be my true attitude, and I believe I should strive to be a demonstration of this confession on a consistent basis.

Let me challenge you to get in touch with who you are and what you believe down deep inside. If you haven't experienced it already, there will come a time when you will feel unwound inside. It happens to all of us. There's nothing more important in life than being centered in Christ. When I was a teenager, on occasion my father and I would talk about what I wanted to be when I grew up. I had so many dreams of traveling all over the world, going to college, singing professionally, having a career, being in the corporate world, learning other languages, etc., etc. The list went on forever. And when I'd tell this to my dad, he would always say, "Honey, as long as you center your will in the will of God, I believe you can do anything you want to. You can go anywhere or become anything you want to become. The most important thing in the world is being centered in God's will." I never forgot that, and when I have consciously sought to do it, it's made all the difference.

Every now and then, I think about putting that center line back on my world globe. In fact, I took it out of its plastic bag not long ago, rolled the world into where my desk was, and attempted to glue it back on. It was hard to do. I couldn't glue it on all the way around. It sagged here and there, ruffled up in other places, fit unevenly. So I finally gave up and put it back in the plastic bag and into the desk drawer. I must open that drawer twenty times a day, and with every opening now, I rather like seeing it there. It helps me remember whose I am and the value of that gift from God. I was bought with a very high price, and I don't ever want to forget it. And every day that I go about my life, I want to be aware that God can keep me in the center of His will. My father was right—that's the most important thing in the world. I can never lose my center nor unravel, as long as I am centered in Him.

May GOD, our very own God, continue to be with us just as he was with our ancestors—may he never give up and walk out on us. May he keep us centered and devoted to him, following the life path he has cleared, watching the signposts, walking at the pace and rhythms he laid down for our ancestors.

—1 KINGS 8:57–58 MSG

19

Under His Wings

SHEILA WALSH

Those who live in the shelter of the Most High will find rest in the shadow of the Almighty. This I declare of the LORD: He alone is my refuge, my place of safety; he is my God, and I am trusting him. For he will rescue you from every trap and protect you from the fatal plague. He will shield you with his wings. He will shelter you with his feathers. His faithful promises are your armor and protection. Do not be afraid of the terrors of the night, nor fear the dangers of the day, nor dread the plague that stalks in darkness, nor the disaster that strikes at midday. . . . The LORD says, "I will rescue those who love me. I will protect those who trust in my name. When they call on me, I will answer; I will be with them in trouble. I will rescue them and honor them. I will satisfy them with a long life and give them my salvation."

—PSALM 91:1–6, 14–16 NLT

When my son Christian was in third grade, he asked if he could go with a friend to a one-week residential Christian camp. I made a few inquiries from other moms whose children had been at this particular camp and they all gave it rave reviews. I talked with Christian's friends mom and we checked availability for the one week her son was free. There was space left so we booked the boys in. We packed his trunk with everything the camp recommended, including five costumes for the theme nights, and when the day arrived we set off. I asked Christian how he was feeling about being away from home for a week, and he said that he was a bit nervous but excited too. As we drove through the gates of the property, all the camp counselors were lined up on each side jumping up and down, welcoming each child to camp. Christian's only comment was, "No more caffeine for them today!"

We checked out his cabin and Christian chose a bunk. "I think I'll wait for my friend to get here before I do anything else, Mom," he said.

"Why don't we go to the registration desk and see if he's checked in?" I suggested.

We discovered that his friend had arrived but there had been a mix-up in the accommodations, and Christian and his friend were in different cabins. He was so disappointed, as was I. I told him that if he felt uncomfortable staying I would totally understand and we could go home but he said no, he'd like to meet the boys that he would be with. The other six boys seemed very friendly and he liked his camp counselor, Partybiz. (Apparently his nick-name referred to his mullet haircut—business in the front, party in the back!) Christian decided that he would stay. Each camper had to take a swim test before they would be given pool privileges, so I watched as Christian performed his most flamboyant dive off the side of the pool.

I left a letter for each day and three camper packages. When it was time to go, he gave me a big hug, told me he'd be fine, and set off with two boys to check out the rest of camp. The moms and dads were given a CD as they exited the camp to listen to on the drive home. It included a mes-sage from the president of the camp, a personal message from your child's counselor, and a short talk on raising healthy kids. I found the CD very helpful and was doing just fine until I was safely home and it got dark!

I can't remember why Barry wasn't home that week-end but for whatever reason he was out of town. We only had one dog at that time, so as I took Belle out for her last walk of the night, I suddenly became aware of every movement in the trees and the funny shadows that they cast. By the time I got home I could hardly breathe. All I could think was, *I just left my sweet little boy in the middle of the woods with a bunch of strangers who say they are Christians, but how do I know?!* As I read this now I think,

Well, how silly is that. I have totally grown as a parent with trust in God and in my son. Well, that's what I would have thought—until yesterday.

Christian is about to go into seventh grade, yes, four years further down the pike. He and two of his friends decided that it would be fun to go to camp together. So once again I went through all the things one does to ensure one's son a place at camp. I checked, double-checked, and re-checked that all three boys were assigned to the same cabin and we set off. It's about a two-hour drive but Barry likes to leave so early that we almost caught the last day of the previous camp. We stopped for lunch and we were still two hours early. Finally the gates opened and we drove in between all the hooting and hollering. We found Christian's cabin and in just a few moments both his friends joined us. They did their swim test and all seemed well. I handed in his care packages and his allergy meds and after big hugs Barry and I set off home listening to our new camp CD.

"Just think," Barry said, "we could see a different movie every night."

"I know, and we can go out for dinner to all the places we like," I added.

"And sleep late!" he said.

We looked at each other and unleashed at the same

moment, "We just left our son in the middle of the woods with a bunch of strangers who say they are Christians but how do we know that?!"

I am coming to realize that this whole being-a-parent thing will always tear at my heart. Christian is growing into a wonderful young man, but we live in a crazy world and we don't know from one moment until the next what is going to happen to us or to those we love. When that reality hits me hard that's when I pull my heart back under the shelter of God's wings because he does know. He knows what will happen today and tomorrow and he has promised that he will be there. He has not promised that we will be spared from pain but that he will be present in the pain.

One of my favorite words is *refuge*. I love it because Christ is our refuge in any storm, large or small. He is our safe haven, our sanctuary. I have six more days of Christian's camp to get through, but you may have eighteen months of a son's or husband's tour of duty to get through. If you are like me, some days the load feels pretty light and you have a firm conviction that God is in control and watching out for those we love. But there are those other days, days when you are tired or discouraged and all the old fears come flooding back. What do you do on those days? This is what I do. I find a quiet place and in my mind. I take

Christian and I imagine that I am placing him right under the shelter of God's wings. It's hard to grasp on this side of heaven how held we are by the love of God, but if only we would lean back and find his wings are strong.

I may have to imagine placing Christian there but the truth is that he is always there. I just have to remember. I pray today that you will know the peace of God, which passes our human grasp, and the love of Christ our Savior that would fill every space of doubt and fear.

20

A Christmas Surprise

✒ MARY GRAHAM

t was Ann Kimmel who used to say, "I love the word *impossible*." I love that word too. It energizes me. And I love the word *community*. There's something about the word that always makes me smile. Growing up in a very small community was wonderful. My parents knew everyone and they all knew us. The entire town felt like our neighborhood and, until I graduated from high school, I cannot remember ever seeing an adult anywhere who didn't call me by name.

Now I live in a small community (although in a very large metroplex) where I don't know everyone, but I'm surrounded by people I know well and love dearly. One of the advantages of such a community, both as a child and now as an adult, is that when you face the impossible, it makes such a difference when you're surrounded by loved ones. When those two realities collide, there is magic in the air and suddenly, even before you see it, you know everything is going to be all right.

Such a "collision" happened when Marilyn Meberg bought a house around the corner from me several years ago. Marilyn and I have been friends since the mid 1970s. She's been a soul mate, a confidante, a counselor, and an incredible friend. We've traveled the world and almost every inch of America together. Although we've traveled with other friends, I always want her in the mix. She's there when I need her, delightfully funny, the best conversationalist, and so fun to know. She's the one to whom my secrets are confided and with whom my problems are discussed. When she bought the house around the corner from me, I was jubilant.

Marilyn's house needed some renovation work before she could move in, but we all begged her to be here before Christmas. That deadline was very tight. She was in California to oversee the packing of her household items, and Ney agreed to oversee the work on her house here. If everything went perfectly as planned, she'd arrive in Dallas on Friday, December 17. Her furniture from California would arrive on Saturday, December 18. And her son and his wife were arriving from California for their Christmas celebration on Monday afternoon, December 20. Christmas, we decided, could stay on December 25.

This was the plan, but it wasn't until about noon on December 17 that the words *impossible* and *community* met in a wonderful explosion and the fun began. No one anticipated or even thought about the plan that began to emerge. We were available, certainly, to help in any way we could, but none of us could have imagined what was about to happen, nor how much fun we would have, nor the kind of joy we were about to experience.

Somehow, Luci Swindoll, Ney Bailey, and Sheila and Barry Walsh and I arrived at Marilyn's newly finished and ready-to-move-in house shortly after noon on Friday. The house was completely empty, perfectly clean, and ready for Marilyn to arrive in about eight hours. There was nothing to do, nothing to be done, except wait for our friend. To this day I don't know exactly what happened. None of us can remember who said what, or if anyone had an idea, or if anyone was even thinking about anything. We were just there. And Marilyn would be soon. We were all very excited about that because she was moving into the neighborhood where we all live. At some point, a moving truck pulled up from a local furniture store. Apparently Marilyn had made a purchase of a bed and a sofa before she left and asked that it arrive before her other furniture.

When those two pieces of furniture came into the house it changed everything. Suddenly we all began to feel enthusiastic about turning that house into a home.

I think I was the one who said to the delivery guy, "What else do you have in the truck? Anything we could see?" What an absolutely ridiculous request. (Which is why I think I am the one who asked!) He said, "Oh, we got a couple things going back to the store." So Barry and I got in the back of the truck and started picking out stuff. Brand new furniture! We found a kitchen table with chairs, a couple of end tables, and a living room chair or two. I knew the owner of the store, having made purchases there myself, and I called her and asked if we could keep the furniture for a couple days and see if Marilyn liked it. If she did, I thought she'd certainly buy it. How ridiculous is that? (I'm not recommending this as common practice.)

Marilyn, we decided, needed a dining room table, so we asked the delivery guys for one of those (also in the truck!). And, there was a beautiful rug in there so we asked for that for the living room, and, I can't remember for sure, but I think we also got one for under the kitchen table. It needed something too. And a few lamps for a little indirect lighting. The furniture guys looked at us like we were idiots, and we were acting like it. All of us were laughing our heads off, calling the owner of the store, and placing furniture here and there. We were like children in a toy store, so caught up with the wonder of what we were creating we lost all sense of reality. (Again, I'm not recommending this as common practice! Even for us it was highly unusual.)

Once the furniture was placed, that house really began to take shape and seem inviting. We had a couple chairs in the entryway, and it was looking great. Then someone got the idea to put up a Christmas tree. Luci had one in her garage she was planning to decorate but hadn't yet. She said, "I'll go get it." Sheila had run an errand, so we phoned her on her cell phone and told her to bring ornaments home to put on the tree. After, "You want me to do what?" she laughed that wonderful laugh of hers and set out on a mission. But now we were running out of time. Marilyn's plane would be arriving within the hour. We kept phoning Sheila at the store to say, "Hurry!" She kept saying, "This takes time!" When she came, we hurriedly decorated the darling tree. She'd picked up a few Christmas candles and she lit them all. Ney went home and got a CD player so we could have Christmas music; we ordered a few pizzas, and called the person picking up Marilyn at the airport to say, "Don't tell her we called, but how close are you?" (We actually made that same call several times.)

About seven o'clock in the evening, right on schedule, the car with Marilyn pulled into the driveway. She was very surprised to find us there. The house was adorable. She was expecting empty space and she found a party. No one is ever more appreciative or verbal than Marilyn, but this time she was speechless. She was delighted, of course, but not more so than we. She's talked about it ever since.

By Saturday morning she had phoned the furniture store and replaced or returned a few things, but that was okay. When her moving trucks came, we were all there to hurriedly help her settle everything. By the time her children arrived Monday afternoon, we were done. She received it all beautifully but the real joy was in the giving. We'll never forget those days of joy and celebration. The task was impossible but the community made it enjoyable, fun, and unforgettable. As bonded as we all were before that, we've been much more bonded since. Marilyn didn't ask for help. We didn't feel any sense of obligation to work for her. We simply got caught up in a great idea that energized us to participate in the work our friend had to do. She could have lived with moving boxes for weeks, and that would've been so understandable. But we got to experience the joy of a nice house, and so did she.

It's such a principle to live by, well founded in the teachings of Jesus himself. Jesus said, "It is more blessed to give than to receive" (Acts 20:35 NIV). And sometimes that blessing is just completely over-the-top. We can kill ourselves worrying about what's wrong and what we're missing. Or we can open our hearts to all the resources God has for us. What do you need? A great idea? A little time? Some energy? His resources are absolutely unlimited. And when you have an opportunity to give to someone else, whether it's time, energy, or money, it always comes back to you. You can never be shortchanged.

21

A Song of Your Own

SANDI PATTY

was so blessed to grow up in a musical family. My dad was a minister of music, and my mother was an amazing pianist, so music was something with which our family was very familiar. We would often sing together when driving, and when we were younger, we would all join in on the melody, but as we got older, we would find ourselves attempting to sing harmony. I use the word *attempting* because when we tried it out the first time, our parents thought we were singing off-key until they realized what we were trying to do. And then, with much encouragement from them, we continued to "attempt" to sing harmony until our "ears" found the right notes. Many hours we spent in the car singing and harmonizing.

When I was in high school, my parents' dream came

true as our family began to record albums and travel across the country singing in different churches. Our first recording was called appropriately *A Dream Come True*, followed by *From Our House to Yours* and *Harmony in Music and Life*. We spent many hours on the road and many hours setting up and tearing down our equipment at numerous churches. Many hours napping, laughing, arguing, and yes, singing in the car.

I have always loved music and I have always loved singing. My parents said that I always seemed to have a song. At the age of five they gave me my very own little 45 rpm record player. I can remember listening to my records night after night and pretending my hairbrush was a microphone. I would sing and dance for hours in my bedroom in front of the mirror. At six, my song was stolen from me when I was sexually abused by a female family friend. Sexual abuse rips the sacred right out of a child. And while I still was very active in music and in singing, I had lost my song.

I began to cover up the pain in my life with many things—food, weight obsession, and even music. I think I hid behind the music. I had a real love/hate relationship with music and singing. I resented it because I thought it was expected of me, and yet I was comfortable in it because it became my identity. I truly felt no one would like me if it weren't for my music. It is something that I still battle in my life from time to time. I often wonder, *Do you really like me for me or just for my music?* So I had to find something else with which to find my identity. My fame? Being a mother? Being an artist? But slowly, as God continues to woo me closer and closer to his heart, I realize that the only identity that matters is who I am in him.

Recently I was doing some research online about music and identity, and I came across a site called DNA Music. OK, this definitely got my attention. I came across a Dr. David Deamer, who is a professor of chemistry at the University of California in Santa Cruz. Dr. Deamer asserts that we all have a unique signature of music within us that comes directly from our DNA. DNA is that "signature" within us that makes us uniquely us. There are no two DNA that are exactly alike—much like a fingerprint or a snowflake, DNA is unique and never copied. That is so fascinating to me.

He says that if you take our DNA chain, which looks to me kind of like a Slinky, and turn it on its side horizontally, you can see the wave patterns. When you take those DNA wave patterns and plug that information into a computer (that is so out of my knowledge level), those wave patterns make sound waves. And those sound waves make music. And that music creates a song.

What he is saying—don't miss this!—is that within each and every one of us is a unique song, given to us by the God of the universe. From the moment of our conceptions, each of us has been singing praises to our heavenly Father. A song, unlike no other. How cool is that?

This is my song to sing in any season—good or bad. Dark or light. Rejoicing or weeping. This song never changes. It is the song of the redeemed, of the loved, of the forgiven, of the cherished. It is the most beautiful song in the universe to my God's ear because he put it there. He created it. And he is crazy about *me*. If that doesn't put you over the top, I don't know what will!

Oh yes, you shaped me first inside, then out;
you formed me in my mother's womb.
I thank you, High God—you're breathtaking!
Body and soul, I am marvelously made!
I worship in adoration—what a creation!
You know me inside and out,
you know every bone in my body;
You know exactly how I was made, bit by bit,
how I was sculpted from nothing into something.
Like an open book, you watched me grow from conception to
*   birth;*

all the stages of my life were spread out before you,
The days of my life all prepared
before I'd even lived one day.

— Psalm 139:13–16 msg

Part 4

22

Over-the-Top Friends

✎ SHEILA WALSH

> *Each person is given something to do that shows who God is:*
> *Everyone gets in on it, everyone benefits. All kinds of things*
> *are handed out by the Spirit, and to all kinds of people! The*
> *variety is wonderful.*

—1 CORINTHIANS 12:7–8 MSG

July 5 is my birthday, and so each year it's a bit of a challenge to organize getting together with my friends in a way that doesn't interfere with any other patriotic parties. In 2009, America's big Fourth of July holiday fell on a Saturday, and as I was driving my son, Christian, to camp on the fifth, my friends decided to have a party for me on the fourth. It was kind of a "God bless America and thank you for the woman with the funny accent" party. They asked me if I wanted to go out for dinner but I opted for having them all here in my home. As we spend a good part of the year traveling and eating endless meals in hotel restaurants, it is a treat to just be at home. So with that agreed upon, my friends told me to do nothing but shower and they would provide the food and beverages.

I was very grateful that they were providing the food, but I decided to do a little decorating to mark our national holiday. I drove to our local party store and picked out fourteen balloons. Two of the balloons were the huge Mylar (foil) type that had USA spelled out on red, white, and blue stars attached to each other. The rest were just regular latex balloons, four of each of the colors of our flag. I don't know if you have ever tried to get fourteen balloons in your car when the temperature is over 100 degrees and there is quite a brisk breeze, but it is a challenge. Before I even got to the car one of the Mylar balloons was headed to Oklahoma. I considered going back for another, but as I was already fighting a buffalo herd of the remaining balloons I decided against it. Two of the plain balloons popped as I tried to negotiate them into the backseat, but I pressed on. I made it home safely without being completely immersed in latex, but as I welcomed them into the cool air of my kitchen, two more popped. This would not have been a huge problem, if it were not for the fact that every balloon that popped was blue. As I arranged them to hang on the door and mailbox, I realized that it looked as if I were celebrating Japan. I have nothing against Japan, but it didn't really seem as if it should be its day, so I returned to the store to re-patriotize my bunch.

At six o'clock my friends arrived, absolutely laden with food of every kind. They had salads and cheeses and chicken and bread and fruit and the yummiest chocolate cake conjured up in one's imagination. As we always do, we sat around and talked and talked and laughed. I looked around the table and was struck again by what each one of these women means to me. There was Mary Graham, president of Women of Faith. We have been friends for almost thirteen years and she has been a steady rock for my family. She has walked and wept with us through the loss of William and Eleanor, Barry's parents. She held Christian when he was a tiny baby, before I realized I would need a nanny to be with him while I was onstage. (I think I thought I could just rock him as I talked!) We have crossed challenging terrain together, always spoken the truth to one another, and have come out the other side stronger friends.

There was also Marilyn Meberg, one of the funniest and wisest women I know. I think my favorite thing about Marilyn is that I know I can tell her anything; I can trust her with my most vulnerable moments in life knowing I will be loved and received not judged. We also share a significant impediment—we laugh like two Clydesdale horses. I value that in her as one never wants to be the only horse in a room laughing.

Then there was the one and only Luci Swindoll. I have never met anyone like Luci before in my life. For a start, she is a wonder in her infectious passion for life and music and art. She is seventy-six years old but you would never know that. She loves to travel and has visited all seven continents, and I would have to say, she lives the life out of every day. When we are traveling together, if something goes wrong, Luci finds a way to make it fun. She also attempted to teach my son to smoke with a breadstick, while playing the piano when he was four years old—not a trick to show his grandmother!

Pat Wenger was there too. Pat has traveled with Marilyn since Women of Faith's inception, and I adore her. My two favorite things about Pat are that she is a wise and caring therapist and the mother of two grown boys. Her sons are married now with children of their own and they all, daughters-in-law included, love her deeply and fight to see who "gets her" for holidays. I continue to learn from Pat, as my son gets bigger with every passing moment.

Finally there was Ney Bailey. We affectionately refer to her as the fourth person of the Trinity. I realize that sounds desperately sacrilegious, but all we mean is she is the one person we all know who is so like Christ in all her ways. She is tender and wise and strong and full to running over with the love of God. Ney has prayed with me through some of the most difficult days of my life and always reminds me that I can never slip from the caring hands of my heavenly Father.

As I looked around my kitchen table and listened in, I saw the common threads in all my friendships with these women: they all make me laugh. We are big believers in the importance of laughter. We all believe in the power of prayer and have spent countless hours together praying. Not one of us views it as a last resort but the first place to fall in the best of times and the worst of times. We firmly believe in loyalty and stand with and for each other. We would rather sit around a table and talk than almost anything else, and we love to give each other gifts. Money is never the point. Some of my most precious gifts from Luci are little drawings that she has done for me. One weekend I said, "Rats!" onstage and by the time the weekend was over, she had drawn the most precious picture of a loyal band of rats. I have it framed in my office! We understand we need each other and trust one another to open up our more vulnerable selves.

We are not designed to do this journey alone; we are not equipped for everything we will need. That's why Christ put us in a "body." I can't imagine what it will be like when we are finally home and all our relationships will be free from the curse of sin. Then there will be no more fear or woundedness. But, until then, we have each other. Treasure your friends. Take time not just to tell them you love them but why you love them, and just imagine what it will be like when our companionship takes us all the way home.

23

Live Generously

🕮 LUCI SWINDOLL

On May 8 my friend Agnes sent me an electronic birthday greeting card—one of those beautiful Jacque Larson e-cards. I'm somewhat familiar with them, but this was the prettiest one I'd seen. I was thrilled. It pictured an easel with a very appealing little watercolor painting of potted plants, flowers, and a white wicker chair. On the floor next to the ease was a palette of paint and a bucket of water. Sitting in midair was the paintbrush. The note to the left read, *"Click on the paint-brush to start"* so, when I did, the brush flew across the scene, with a black daub of paint on the tip of the brush, and added a little kitty into the watercolor. As music played in the background, the brushstrokes kept doing their work. The kitty jumped in and out of the painting, playing with a ball of yarn, drinking milk, and finally plopping on a pillow that had been painted on the chair to sleep. Right at the bottom was a sweet note from Agnes with her birthday wishes. The whole thing was so well done I watched it several times.

But, here's what's interesting—it wasn't my birthday. When I opened the e-mail from Agnes, I realized she'd gotten the day right, but the month wrong. My birthday is September 8, not May 8. She'd forgotten my exact birthday, but she *remembered me*.

Have you ever stopped to consider all the people in the world that nobody remembers? There are millions. They have no one who cares, thinks about, or misses them. They never get a smile of recognition or a kiss good night, much less a warm greeting card from a friend. I've seen children in India whose parents died of AIDS and those in Africa who've lost their closest loved ones in the horror of genocide. They are completely alone. And we don't have to go to another country to find people without love or hope or companionship. All we have to do is look down the street or walk through the neighborhood right where we live.

On May 9, Agnes wrote me another note. This time, it was an apology for not getting the month right. I responded immediately and told her there was no need to apologize. I absolutely *loved* the card and it was the only birthday greeting I got that day. It didn't matter that it wasn't my birthday—what mattered was that she thought about me and sent her love in that clever, unforgettable way.

For years I've said, "Take everything as a compliment and you'll live longer." You'll stop feeling sorry for yourself and you'll be a lot happier. I don't know very many people who do that, but I promise you, if you try it for a while, it'll change your mental health. Look at what the apostle Paul said in 1 Thessalonians 5:16–18, "Be cheerful no matter what; pray all the time; thank God no matter what happens. This is the way God wants you who belong to Christ to live" (MSG).

For a number of years now I've been troubled with arthritis in my knees, especially the right one. There's no cartilage left, so the knee bones rub together when I stand, walk, sit, or kneel. Sometimes I can even hear my knees knocking, like I'm part of a scary movie. Finally, in the summer of 2008, I decided to go to an orthopedic surgeon to find out what it would take to make me feel better, or perhaps have that knee replaced with an artificial one. I knew I had a full schedule of travel with Women of Faith coming up and was seventy-five years old. Those two things alone gave me pause. Should the doctor prescribe surgery, when did I think I was going to have it? I asked my dear friend Mary Graham to go with me in case I didn't remember everything he said. (I not only needed another knee, but another mind.) She very graciously agreed and off we went to Medical City to see Dr. Charles Rutherford, a joint replacement surgeon.

I liked him a lot—serious, kind, to-the-point, and realistic. His nurse had me weigh and took a few X-rays, the results of which were passed on to the doctor. As we talked about my knees, how long I had felt this way, my questions regarding a possible surgery, etc., Dr. Rutherford said, "You know, Luci, even if you have surgery, the first thing you need to do is lose eighty pounds. You have to get the weight off your knees. Can you do that?"

"Yes," I immediately responded, and meant every word. "That's a lot to lose, but I can do it. Then, will I have surgery after that?"

"We'll see," he said. "Let's get the weight-bearing mass off first, then we'll evaluate things again and decide what's best to do. I could give you an artificial knee now, but with your weight, the pain might be gone for only six months. I'd rather you get the weight off first so the surgery would be effective for a longer period of time."

The minute I got in the car that day, I said to Mary, "Just think about what that doctor told me. Isn't that *great* news? Here I am in my seventies. I know countless people my age who go to the doctor every single day and are told they have cancer. Or, they've got a brain tumor. Or, their diabetes is so bad they'll never walk again or they have the beginning of Alzheimer's. And this guy asks me if I can *lose weight*? Are you kidding me? This is fabulous. Savor this moment, honey. I've got it made."

On the way home from the doctor's office that day, we stopped at a bookstore and I bought *Atkins for Life*. Dr. Rutherford had encouraged me to start the Atkins diet and also to buy a recumbent bike. That very day I went on that diet, checked into buying the bike, and within a month had begun both losing weight and maintaining an exercise program.

About eight months later I went back to see the doctor, have him record my progress, and thank him for possibly saving my life. And do you know what he told me? He said, "Since you were in here last June, Luci, you've lost a significant amount of weight." (At that point, it was forty-eight pounds.) "But what's interesting is that I've had maybe sixty patients come in here with the identical problem as yours, and I gave them the same instructions. But, there have been only two people who have lost the weight. You're one of them. I'm proud of you."

What would have happened had I not taken that

diagnosis as a compliment? *But Luci, you had to lose the weight*, you might be thinking. *That wasn't a compliment. It was a diagnosis. It had to do with your health, not your feelings.* That's my whole point! What about the fifty-eight people who didn't lose weight? What was their excuse? Were they offended by being told they needed to? It's how we receive things mentally that determines our response. In the example with the birthday card, I could have thought, *Gosh! This is my friend. You'd think she could at least get my birthday right.* But, when we receive everything as a gift instead of an offense, we are able to view things as a blessing, not a penalty.

I think it's very easy to be offended in today's world. I know people who love to get their feelings hurt. The slightest thing offends them—being left out, being interrupted, others not keeping their word, misunderstandings, and more. It's as if the person wants others to be completely responsible for how they feel—*If you hurt my feelings you owe me something.* I know this because I, too, can feel that way when I let myself. We feel taken advantage of or misunderstood, so we pout, want to run away, need to withdraw. It's very easy to feel this way. What's *not* easy is to let it go and take it as a compliment . . . as an opportunity to grow.

One of my favorite verses in Psalms is found in chapter 119, verse 165. It reads, "Those who love your teachings will find true peace, and nothing will defeat them" (NCV). Or, the way I learned it as a kid was, "Great peace have they which love thy law: and nothing shall offend them" (KJV). Personally, I would love to live that way every day—believing that verse and applying it in my life. If we could do that, we'd have more peace, sweeter fellowship with others, and an ongoing, vibrant communication with the Lord.

And for those of you who get easily offended, how about trying this: "And if someone takes unfair advantage of you, use the occasion to practice the servant life. No more tit-for-tat stuff. Live generously." Matthew wrote that (5:42 MSG). I bet anything it worked for him.

24

The Walk of Life

✎ SANDI PATTY

I f there is one thing that I dread most in my life, it is the need to walk for twenty minutes four to five days a week. I don't know what it is about it, but I just can't get up off my rear end and do it. When I put it down on paper it doesn't seem like much at all. Twenty minutes—that's not even as long as a sitcom; it's definitely not as long as a soap opera, and I don't seem to have trouble finding the time for that. Honestly, I know it is a much deeper issue for me than just the twenty minutes of walking. It somehow hits at a core issue for me, and that is failure. Yes, failure. I think I set these unrealistic goals for myself and then don't follow through because I "know" that I will fail. So, instead of trying, I just self-prophesy and fail before I even start.

I don't know if that makes sense to you, but somehow

it makes sense to me. I try to self-talk, encourage myself, do some self-motivating, but it just doesn't work. I guess I carry a message deep within myself—why try something if I am only going to fail? I would never allow my children to be okay with that message. I would say to them something like, "Set realistic goals," or "Doing something is better than doing nothing." But to let them be okay with telling themselves that they shouldn't even try because they are going to fail? That's just not okay.

I want to be fit and thin right now. I think that is the other inner message I struggle with. I am so all about immediate gratification—I don't know how to "work toward" something. I mean, I know in my head, but to be disciplined enough to really know it in my inner being—I just can't seem to get there. Even now, as I am writing this devotional, I wonder if it is some kind of ruse to get out of walking twenty minutes today. I have the time; I have the opportunity. But to get up, put on my tennis shoes, and go walk starts to give me anxiety. I start breathing hard; my heart begins to race. *What is this all about?* It's wild. It's only twenty minutes. *C'mon!* Now I'm getting frustrated with myself.

You know, what I *ought* to do is get my shoes on, go walk, and then come back and finish this devotional. Great idea . . . so, why am I still sitting here? Okay, I'm gonna do it. It is now 1:06 p.m.—see you in twenty minutes or so. *Help!* . . .

Well, I'm back and it is 1:30 p.m.—the next day. What on earth happened? Well, I was hoping you would ask. It's like this. I got up, got my tennis shoes on, and began walking. I walked for a while and wanted to see how long I had been walking, so I looked at my watch, only to realize I had forgotten to bring it. So I had no idea how long I had been walking and couldn't time my entire walk. Drama! As I kept walking, I began to look at my surroundings. It was beautiful here in Indiana. Although Don, Sam, Mollie, and I currently live in Oklahoma City, we are visiting in Anderson so we can see the other kids and parents. The weather was gorgeous.

I kept walking and kept enjoying the surroundings, when suddenly it hit me. I have been focusing on the wrong thing. I have been focusing on the accomplishment, on the goal, and I was missing the journey. I kept hearing that still small voice within me (most definitely God in my life) saying, "Sandi, just enjoy the walk." I do that with so many things in my life—I set these goals and expectations about something, and then I miss the joy of the moment. This moment was huge for me. To just get out and walk, not to see if my heart rate was up or how long I would walk or how far. But just to *enjoy the walk*. How very simply profound.

During my walk, my cell phone rang, which I carry with me at all times in case the kids call. (I call my cell phone my umbilical cord because it keeps me attached to my kids). Anyway, one of the kids called and needed to talk, and it was wonderful to just listen. I was enjoying the walk and the talk so much that I completely lost track of time. When I finally got back to the condo and looked at the clock, I realized that I had walked not for twenty minutes, but one hour and twenty minutes! And I enjoyed almost every minute of it. God has such a great sense of humor, doesn't he? God is teaching me to enjoy the journey—with him right by my side. Imagine that!

25

The Lighter Side of Life

  PATSY CLAIRMONT

> *Laughter is the spark of the soul.*
>
> — ANON

My friends are such fun! I hope you have a truck-load of those because they help us survive. They are the kind that inspire you to laugh out loud when they aren't even trying. They keep the happy sparks flying. Take my friend who was coming over for a visit recently but ran into a delay, so she sent me the following text . . . "Running late . . . I lost my bra."

Do you find that as humorous as I do? For her it was reality, for me it was relief. There's just something about predicaments we find ourselves in that can be honking funny.

Take my girlfriend Leslie who loves to take walks in the cemetery. (I didn't say my friends are normal. I said they are funny.) The other day she was stepping right along in an attempt to work off dessert when her cell phone rang. She didn't want to lose stride so she chatted and walked with aerobic purpose, but soon Leslie was so caught up in the conversation she didn't notice exactly where she was going . . . until she heard an unfamiliar sound.

First came a flapping noise, like someone briskly shaking out sheets on a windy day, followed by an exaggerated hissing, like a pent-up radiator letting off steam. Leslie looked up only to discover she had walked smack dab into a flock of grazing Canadian geese . . . and one of the big daddy geese wasn't feeling hospitable toward drop-in guests. To prove his displeasure with this intruder's presence, he decided to make known his disdain in a memorable way.

With a great flurry of determination the race was on when the male Canadian goose began chasing the female fleeing Leslie. She wasn't sure which could be heard the farthest the giant bird's hoarse honking or her girly screeching. Leslie told me later she had no idea that a web-footed bird could run faster than she who was cinched securely into her pink high-tops. She had to make some strategic running back moves, darting between grave sites before the bird, dizzy from Leslie's headstone-hopscotching, finally returned to his gaggle . . . probably for a good giggle, as he watched the sprinting lady hightail it for home. Initially Leslie had all the ha-ha knocked out of her regarding her "experience" until a nap revived her fun-loving perspective.

I would have gladly paid to watch that video.

Another friend confessed that recently she went into a public restroom and into a stall. The toilet tissue holder was broken and was missing the outside cover, which held the inner workings in place. The roll of tissue, obviously meant to last for a large crowd, was the size of a wagon wheel and was threaded on a short peg. When my friend needed the paper, she tugged on the tissue with more gusto than she meant to, causing the wheel of paper to spin off the peg, hit the floor, roll under the door, and across the bathroom floor. She felt her face (excuse the expression) flush. A stranger called out, "Lose something, honey?" My friend stood still and held her breath, hoping folks might think it had rolled out from under a different stall, when she realized she was still holding the initial tail of the tissue, and it was still securely attached to the streamer that was affixed to the roll. This meant the evidence led definitively to her.

Laughter is the shortest distance between two people.

—Victor Borge

My friends Nancy and David are a playful and popular couple. They have a delightful combination of humor and devotion. They usually are a harmonious couple but on rare occasions they will have a tiff. Early on in their marriage they had one of those moments . . . that lasted three days.

David, the mellower one of the two, had a negative response toward Nancy who had made a decision on his behalf that he didn't appreciate. Nancy felt he was being silly when after a couple of silent days they still weren't speaking. She was aware David was getting ready to leave for a business trip the following morning and Nancy knew he would come to her first and apologize. But he didn't, and as the evening progressed, it became obvious to her that he wasn't going to. This really aggravated Nancy and she decided to seek some sweet revenge. So she slipped into their room, while David was involved in a TV show, and opened his packed suitcase. Nancy then carefully slipped out his stack of underwear he had neatly packed and replaced them with a note. That night she slept with a grin on her face, and when she awoke, David had already left for the airport.

Upon David's arrival at his hotel he called home. When the phone rang Nancy was hesitant to answer, but she was ready with her defensive reasons for doing such an impish act. Much to her surprise David had called to apologize. When he finished, she asked him sheepishly if he had unpacked yet. He had not. Nancy told him he might want to do that before they hung up. Knowing his wife like he did, David asked, "What did you do?"

Nancy held on the line while David opened his case and read her note. At first the room and phone line were silent, and then David began to laugh, louder and louder. He finally picked up the receiver and they chortled together.

Whew! That was risky, but gratefully their shared love and humor brought them back into unity. Oh, wait, I didn't tell you what the note said . . . "David, your attitude stinks, and now so does your only pair of underwear!"

Mirth is God's medicine. Everybody ought to bathe in it.

—HENRY WARD BEECHER

Yes, there's just something about fun people that helps take the edge off of controversy. Their humor helps decrease tension, relieves stress, and even helps restore peace. We aren't surprised since God thought laughter up for our health. But it is easy to get so pulled into the tough stuff of life we overlook all the reasons tucked inside a day that are funworthy.

My husband Les knows how to pick the pocket of humor. He is one of those fortunate people who wakes up with a smile and quickly turns it into a gift that he gives away to others. Me? Not so much. I have to work my way to funny so I admire my husband's spontaneous light-hearted spirit.

Did I mention that Les is in pain every day? He never has a pain-free hour, but only those of us who are close to him know of his intense levels of discomfort, because he's committed to taking God's medicine . . . a merry heart.

Les's merry heart expresses itself in a myriad of ways. For instance, he has the wildest collection of singing toys that never fails to cause guests to laugh with delight. He has a roller skating bear who sings Edelweiss, a Harley driving Santa Claus who sings "Grandma Got Run over by a Reindeer," a talking fish, a set of dancing, guitar-strumming, singing hamsters, a drumming frog, etc. The menagerie at times gets on my nerves (I mean, how many times can one listen to a hamster sing, "I'm a Yankee Doodle Dandy"?) until I see the unexpected pleasure they bring.

My courageous, outrageous husband inspires me to put on a happy face. Now how about you? Who inspires you not to take yourself so seriously? Who makes you laugh out loud? Are you naturally funny? No? Well, I saw a duck at the drugstore who, when you push his button, laughs insanely. Guaranteed to make you chuckle even if you weren't in a good mood. Too bad it wasn't a Canadian goose . . . I know just who I would give that to.

Honk! Honk!

26

What Were You Thinking?

MARILYN MEBERG

The "What were you thinking?" question has an ancient history. It is not specifically asked of Adam and Eve by an incredulous God, but we can presume the question must have been in the divine mind. *Why did you disobey and throw away perfection? What were you thinking?* The question has been resounding through the corridors of history ever since.

Perhaps the question is asked most often of tweens and teenagers whose behavior at times defies all logic and balanced thinking. I well remember standing confidently in front of Mr. Clark responding to his question, "Are you sure you know how to drive a tractor?" and me saying,

"Absolutely." I was twelve years old, had never even been on a tractor. and knew nothing about driving one. What was I thinking?

I was not thinking beyond my desire to drive that tractor. The idea of my friend Dorothy (Mr. Clark's daughter) and me setting off down the scenic country road behind their house was totally appealing to me. The primary appeal was the anticipated joy of riding in the open air the tractor would provide. Although I did not recognize it then, but know now, I am the convertible type. I love open-air travel. I have a convertible and plan to take it with me into eternity. What glorious fun it will be to breeze around the streets of gold waving at all the loved ones I have not seen in years. (Don't check my theology on this one, but why not?)

The "What were you thinking?" question was posed to me after I told my father that Mr. Clark had said I could drive his tractor. Dad's protestations made no sense to me. I didn't tip it over, drive it too fast, or wonder how to start and stop. And I didn't think I had lied to Mr. Clark when I told him I knew how to drive a tractor—he didn't ask if I had driven a tractor but if I knew how. I thought, *How hard could it be to figure that out when I "board" it?*

Now here's the interesting thing about my seemingly illogical and morally challenged thinking: I was making decisions and defending them with a brain more like a kindergartner's than a pre-adolescent's. Does that mean I am brain-challenged? I was then and refuse to take a vote about now. But some new neuroscience discoveries in the past decade are shedding some light on my "then" and the "thens" of other tweens and teens.

The bottom line from this research is: don't trust your adolescent. Why not? Because their brains are not yet fully developed. It was once thought that brain development was basically complete by age six. Now that MRI scans have become a common research tool, scientists can take a look into teenage brains and come to understand why their behavior reflects a lack of good judgment and they are prone to impulsive risk taking. The brain's gray matter, which forms the bulk of its structure and processing capacity, grows gradually throughout childhood and peaks around age twelve. (I was at my peak when I stood in front of Mr. Clark.) The reason I did not use better moral and ethical judgment is simply that I was "underpruned" at that stage! What? At around age twelve, the brain energetically begins pruning away underused neurons. That pruning begins at the back of the brain and slowly moves forward during adolescence. So the regions that control sensory and motor skills mature first. The part of the brain (the prefrontal cortex) that is responsible for judgment and impulse control matures last. In fact, the prefrontal cortex is often not "done" until the early twenties.

So if I had been twenty years old when I stood in front of Mr. Clark, I would have spoken to him with a fully developed prefrontal cortex. Instead of saying I knew how to drive his tractor, I would have told him I had never been on a tractor. I might have assured him, however, that based on my fully developed prefrontal cortex, I would know not to drive too fast or turn corners too sharply, and I would be aware of the chickens mindlessly crossing the road in front of me.

So this is what we need to know about the question "What were you thinking?": we need to keep a sharp but loving eye on our adolescent kids and understand they may not have a clue how to answer the question "What were you thinking?" That requires patience for parents and whoever else is working with young people. The reason for that is simply their prefrontal lobe, which houses the processing capabilities for determining what is wise and unwise, has yet to be fully developed. What is obviously impulsive and risky behavior to us does not seem so to them.

So for those of you who are parents of tweens and teens, how do you resist the Mark Twain thinking, which was to put kids from the age of twelve to eighteen in a box, feed them, store them, and when they "come of age," release them into the wild commonly known as society? One of the most frightening aspects of parenting comes when the "children" get their driver's licenses—not for a tractor, but for a car! We hardly need to be told that a brain yet to be developed in the areas of risk taking and impulsive behavior can be a menace on the streets.

A sobering statistic is that car accidents are the chief cause of death and disability among teenagers, with teens being killed at four times the rate of adults. However, all is not lost. There is a growing number of solutions. One is a GPS tracking device that senses and records the sights and sounds of any abrupt, potentially risky maneuvers made by a well-meaning but brain-challenged young driver. That tracking device sends an immediate e-mail to parents. Whoops . . . busted! A lower-budget approach, which I frankly find very appealing, is a bumper sticker with a slogan "Call My Mom" and a toll-free number for reporting erratic and unsafe driving. Each sticker contains a unique code number allowing anonymous tips to be quickly forwarded to the appropriate parents.

Of course our teens are going to protest loudly, feel their privacy is invaded, and attempt the usual guilt-producing question, "Why don't you trust me?" The answer is, "I love you too much to risk your having an accident." The answer for you to tell yourself is to stick by your guns and tell them a safe driving record will increase your assurance they are ready to drive. That takes a little time. But remember, you are the parent, not the best friend. There are times when "Because I said so" is perfectly appropriate.

But what about those of us who cannot get by with the "lagging prefrontal cortex" excuse when the "What were you thinking?" question is asked? When any one of us finds ourselves "not thinking beyond our desire"? We, like our teens, need to take Proverbs 3: 21 literally: "Don't lose sight of good planning and insight. Hang on to them, for they fill you with life and bring you honor and respect" (NLT).

While our kids' brains are still developing, we must be vigilant about their safety and steer them ultimately to "good planning." We also have the daunting responsibility to be models of good planning. I guess that means we stay off tractors until age twenty!

27

Linking Arms

✍ MARY GRAHAM

Two are better than one.

— ECCLESIASTES 4:9 NIV

I have always loved this verse and have seen the truth of it every day of my life. But never more than two years ago . . . that was when I did something I had never done, never wanted to do, never intended to do, and cannot even believe I did. Neither did my friends believe it. And what I did was something I absolutely could not have done alone: I participated in a half marathon. I didn't run, but I walked. I didn't intend to do it, didn't want to do it, wasn't forced to do it, but I did it. I knew it was the right thing to do, so I made the commitment. And quite honestly, I've never made a harder nor a better decision. Not only do I feel better, I am better for having done it. And it was against all odds that I dove in. Here's exactly what happened.

My (otherwise) magnificent boss, Mike Hyatt, asked

everyone on his team to compete in a half marathon. (At first I thought, "Can he do that? Do labor laws allow it?" I was being facetious, of course, but it honestly did cross my mind.) I got his e-mail with this request when I was on vacation in Italy, eating pasta smothered in rich, creamy sauces. The suggestion that I actually take on a physical challenge in my immediate future felt very rude, like cruel and unusual punishment. I considered changing careers, and I was with three friends (including Luci Swindoll and Marilyn Meberg) who encouraged that decision. They all thought I should decline, although they didn't actually have strong feelings about anything but my own desires and decisions. They encouraged me to do whatever felt good and right to me. We had long discussions about it as we savored our wonderful meals and rich Roman desserts. I wanted my heart to be open to Mike's request, but I knew if I made the commitment, Marilyn and Luci were right—I had to be self-inspired to do it.

Amazingly, the idea of doing the half marathon just kept coming to my mind, and it was beginning to sound almost inviting. I don't know how it happened, but clearly there was transformation in my thinking that I wasn't engineering. Could it be of God? Could it be the right thing for me and my health? Was this something I really could consider?

Anyone who knows me understands there is not an athletic nor competitive bone in my body. I've never played a sport, nor have I enjoyed any kind of physical activity since jumping rope in the third grade. I was a cheerleader in high school but I did more cheering than anything very athletic. I'm healthy, have great energy, and am very active, which has always felt like exercise enough for me. Even working hard seemed like enough exercise. But after Mike's challenge, I couldn't get this half marathon off my mind. Should I try? Could I do it? Would I find any value in the process? I began to think if someone could help me, maybe I could do it. Never having done anything like this, I thought of a friend who I suspected could coach me through the process, help me know what to do, push me when needed, and pull me through to the end. I e-mailed her from Rome and she graciously became my servant and my leader, all in one fell swoop.

In the e-mail to my friend, Lynn Wittenburg, I remember swearing her to secrecy, being very tentative in my request and desire, but putting the question to her: *If* I decided to do it, and *if* I could do it, could she help me? I frankly didn't know what kind of help I needed, but I knew I couldn't even attempt the challenge without someone telling me what to do and when. The day I returned from vacation I went to an athletic store to buy shoes, which felt much more foreign to me than Italy. I was embarrassed to explain to the adorable clerk (who looked like an Olympic athlete himself) that I had no idea what I needed. He wasn't the least bit intimidated by the challenge.

With new shoes on my feet and fear and trepidation in my heart, Lynn showed up at my door one pre-dawn morning and we walked. A little. I was worn out from the beginning, complained a good bit of the way, and dragged my feet. Lynn kept her energy and smile and was my amazing cheerleader. A few days later we did it again, and later, again, and still later, again and again. From January through most of April, we met at least once a week. Lynn was a saint and an angel in disguise. She knew what to do, how far to go, what pace to keep, and when to place her hand in the small of my back for just that added bit of strength and encouragement. Because she's a runner, she'd often run miles before she ever came to pick me up. She wasn't helping me for her own exercise but because I couldn't do it alone. There were days I'd say I couldn't go another step, and she'd laugh and keep us going. Then there were times I'd say that, and she'd say, "Let's stop." It all felt the same to me, but she understood what I didn't— the difference between my needing a break and my wanting a break.

One Saturday we walked eight miles. I was astonished. Frankly, I was astonished it didn't kill me and I didn't kill Lynn. It got easier as we walked farther and farther every week, but when we actually walked the half marathon, I thought I'd die. I actually did almost pass out when I finished (only because I didn't drink the water I was told to drink along the way). Although I didn't exactly enjoy it and don't plan to ever do it again, I am so grateful for having done it. First of all, I feel so much better, as I've kept up the walking. (Just not so far!) When I'm in an airport or an arena, as I often am, I am so grateful I can walk far and fast without any hesitation.

Notwithstanding the fact that I don't like walking far or fast, I'm fascinated by what I learned in the process about companionship and the grace God provides for us in each other. Lynn could walk (or run) to the moon and back on any given day. If others were going, she could beat them. She knows what to do and how to do it. But she was so sweet to help me. She's half my age and twice the athlete I could ever be or would ever want to be. She helped me know what to do and how to do it. At times she was a cheerleader, and other times she was a coach. But mostly she came alongside and made it possible for me to do (with help) what I could never do alone. Sometimes going up a long hill, I'd feel myself lagging behind and losing pace.

Without saying a word, she'd come beside me, slip her arm through mine, and I would immediately pick up my pace to match hers without even trying! When I'd get back on course, she would slip her arm out and on we'd go, separate but together.

That's when I'd be reminded why God gave us His Holy Spirit—to come alongside us and empower us to do what we cannot do in our own strength. He is our Helper (Jesus said in John 14:16 he would give us another Helper). Nobody knows us better than our heavenly Father, and He is *not* surprised that we not only need help, we need a Helper. And it's why He gave us one another. The Christian life is not designed for Lone Rangers. As believers, we were created for relationship. In relationship, we learn so much about ourselves, our strengths, weaknesses, and needs. We grow. Jesus didn't do life on earth alone and neither should we. When Lynn was out of town, I never wanted to walk. The minute she called me, I was ready to go. My frustration with the process became a positive, "I can do that!" I couldn't have done it alone, but with a friend by my side, the impossible wasn't.

I didn't mind walking 8 miles in a day, or 13.1 for that matter, but I'd still really rather drive. (Isn't that why God made automobiles?) I'm so grateful the experience made me stronger and physically fitter. It's made a big difference in my health and well-being. both physically and emotion-ally. What I'm especially glad I didn't miss, however, is the experience of knowing exactly what it means to have a Helper and to be reminded: two are better than one.

28

Brotherly Love

NICOLE C. MULLEN

We have a tradition in our house much like many other households: whenever one of the kids loses a tooth, they place it under the pillow, go to sleep, and in the morning, *voila!*, the tooth is gone and in its place is a dollar bill. Often this process can take several days in my household because the Tooth Fairy is often late. My kids laugh at me when I make up a lame story about the Tooth Fairy being stuck or caught up somewhere, lost in "outta space." They giggle and say, "Ma, we know it's you," and I'm like, "What, what?" Most of the time they give me a big hug and a smile, letting me know that I have once again been forgiven. When my memory cells start working, not only do I pay up, but also I pay with dividends. Most of the time it's something like an extra dollar per tooth for each late night the Tooth Fairy was tardy . . . that'll teach ya to be late.

One weekend while my daughter Jasmine and I were traveling to one of the Women of Faith conferences, Josiah (my youngest) lost a tooth. Upon returning from our journey, I greeted my sons individually, asking about their "Super Fella Weekend" without the girls. As Josiah spoke to me, I noticed that he had an extra gap in his bottom row of teeth. I said something like "Hey little man, did you lose a tooth?" He smiled and said, "Yes, ma'am." I asked if it hurt, to which he shook his head and let me know that one of his older brothers had actually done the deed.

Later on, over a grilled cheese sandwich, he filled me in on the rest of the details.

"I know that teeth don't turn into dollars, but after Maxwell"—one of his eleven-year-old brothers—"pulled it out for me, I put it under my pillow. And then this morning Maxwell went downstairs, got a dollar, put it under my pillow, and took the tooth. Then woke me up and said, 'Josiah, Josiah, wake up. I think your tooth is gone.' So I checked, and he was right. And there was money there, and my tooth was gone!" he chuckled.

Even with the mystery removed, Josiah was so excited. He didn't mind in the least bit that I had not been there to do it. In that moment, his brother had filled in the gap so he felt loved and celebrated. And somehow, even in knowing the truth of the matter, he still projected a sense of wonder in the tone of his five-year-old voice. As he came to the end of the story (but not the end of the grilled cheese sandwich), I excused myself for a moment and went to verify the tale. I asked my husband David if what Josiah said was true. He affirmed the positive and admitted that he was not even aware that Max had pulled Josiah's tooth until after it was done, and he also confirmed that he himself had not done the "under the pillow swap."

So with tears of joy and motherly pride, I entered the toy room and called for the younger of my two eleven-year-old sons. Once he was in a reachable distance, I opened my arms to him and said as he leaned into me, "Max, did you pull your brother's tooth and then gave him a dollar for it?"

He said yes in a humble way, clearly not expecting for it to be as big of a deal as I was making it. So I placed a kiss on the top of his head and thanked him, telling him how proud I was of him. To that he smiled, hugged me a little tighter, and quietly said, "You're welcome, Mom. It was really no problem." Then he returned to his play, without missing a beat.

I am so proud of the young man that Max is becoming and how he so ungrudgingly extended grace to me by quietly stepping up and filling in my gap. He could have easily passed the buck to his dad, or told Josiah that he would have to wait until "Mommy Tooth Fairy" came back into town. But not only was he punctual (OK, I'm working on it), but he did it for the sheer pleasure of watching someone else express their joy. This reminded me of the scripture that says, "How good and how pleasant it is for brothers to dwell together in unity!" (Psalm 133:1 NASB). I wonder if God smiles with pleasure when we get along with each other. When we are more concerned with helping our brothers and sisters than we are about what we want, what we need. When we would inconvenience ourselves to convenience another? Come to think of it, fewer things make us happier as parents than when we see our children getting along. Laughing. Playing. Sharing. Few things overwhelm us with as much joy as when we see them crossing the line toward true maturity, doing what is right, not just because they are afraid of getting in trouble but because they are truly motivated by love.

Jesus summed up the whole duty of man when he taught us to love the Lord our God with all our hearts, with all our souls, with all our minds, and with all our strength, and to love our neighbor as ourselves. We are to love him with all of our PDA (Passions, Drive, Ambitions). We are to love him with our emotions, thoughts, and energy, and when we are doing this, it is then that we are equipped to love our neighbors as ourselves. If I am committed to regularly feeding and taking care of myself, then that should be the measuring stick I use to take care of the hungry. If I clothe myself with nice things and want to appear before others as presentable, then with the same standard, I should provide for others in need.

My older son Maxwell was motivated to help his brother in a way that my younger son could not help himself. He pulled the tooth of a five-year-old to make way for more permanent, fuller teeth. He was gentle in his amateur extraction, gave Josiah something clean to bite down on 'til the bleeding ceased, and even followed up with gifts. In a similar way, we are called to come alongside those who live among us. There are times when we may need to tell them the truth in love, knowing that it will hurt. But we are not called to just leave them bleeding from our verbal rebukes. It is also our duty to help them heal and grow as we aid them in being disciples of Christ.

My prayer for you, as well as for myself, is that we would truly live out the words of Christ and love those around us—those within our reach as well as those outside of it. Whether they come in the form of family members, strangers, loved ones, or foes, might we inconvenience ourselves to convenience another and give from our resources to bring a smile and fill a need?

Part 5

29

The Touch of the Master

⟐ SANDI PATTY

Some years ago I went on a cruise where passengers had the opportunity to stop at different ports along the way. Some ports were interesting places to go and some, well, let's just say it's just better to stay on the boat during those stops. But one particular port, somewhere in the Caribbean, was so beautiful that I decided to get off for a bit and go exploring. Near the dock was a series of several shops. Some sold jewelry, some perfume, and some were the touristy, T-shirt kind of shops. But there was a little art place that caught my eye. The paintings in the window were so beautiful and captivating I found myself opening the door and going in to explore further.

As I looked around I saw the same painting that was in the window displayed all over the store. There must have been fifty or so of the same Caribbean seascape at sunset. It was truly a beautiful piece. As I got closer to one of the pieces, I noticed that it was almost as perfect as a painting could be. Framed in a lovely complementary frame, it was breathtaking. When I looked at the price, I was shocked that it was so cheap. I think it was something like $25 for a large, framed portrait. I couldn't believe it. It looked so much more expensive.

As I continued to walk around the shop, another piece caught my eye. It was the same painting I had been seeing, but it was different somehow. It was a little rougher in nature—you could see a smudge here and there that the other paintings didn't have. There was no beautiful frame; it was just a canvas with frayed edges. In a way it looked tackier than the other paintings that I had seen that were so perfect and smudgeless. I remember thinking to myself, *Wow, if the others are only $25, this must be $2 or $3.* But to my surprise, the price tag said it was $2000! I couldn't believe it. I thought there must be a mistake on the price tag,

I asked the clerk, "Why are these perfect paintings so much cheaper than this one?"

She quickly and enthusiastically replied, "Oh, it's

because the artist actually touched this canvas with his own hands. The others are just reproductions and have many of the flaws airbrushed out. You see," she continued, "it is the flaws and the imperfections that make it authentic. It is because of those smudges and 'mistakes' that we know it is the real thing. It is the work of the master artist, and the painting is exactly how he created it."

OK, can you say "spiritual analogy" here, or what? I so wanted to buy the more valuable painting, but instead I bought a small reproduction to remind me of that moment. I came away from that art store vowing to myself that I would always strive to be real and authentic, even if that meant my flaws and imperfections would show. There are so many days that I would love to airbrush out so much on the canvas of my life. So many days when I would love to wipe away those imperfections and smudges.

And then I think of the apostle Paul who prayed not once, not twice, but three times in his life for the "thorn in his flesh to be taken away." As Paul talked so much about the process and journey of our faith, I have to believe that it wasn't just three times in the course of five minutes that he prayed this prayer, but in three significant seasons in his life that he poured his heart out to God about his flaws. "Why God, why?" he asked. But as he prayed and wrestled and processed, Paul was able to come to place where he finally said, "OK . . . here is the secret of contentment that I have found. I know what it is like to be flawed, to be hungry and poor. I know what it is like to be needy and to have nothing. I even know what it is like to have stuff—good stuff—in my life. But that is not what brings contentment." (I am seriously paraphrasing here.) He sums up all of this to say, "Here it is. Here is the secret, the key, to abundant life: I can do everything—*everything*—through Him who gives me the strength to do so." (I'm seriously paraphrasing Philippians 4:12–13 here.)

I wish the truth and reality of these verses came as easily as simply typing them here today. I feel like Paul so many times. I pray at different seasons in my life about things I just can't get a handle on—things that seem so easy for someone else, but just plain hard for me. I am still praying that prayer. And even as I am praying that today, I am nudged by Paul's affirmation of faith: "I can, I can, I really can do all things through him [Christ] who gives me the strength to do so."

I pray today that, as you embrace your flaws and imperfections, you will remember and know in your deepest knowing that God is the master artist. You have been touched by his hand—that's what makes you real. It is his touch that makes you authentic, flaws and all. Amen and amen!

30

Not Just *Enough*, but More Than You Can Contain

SHEILA WALSH

> On the final and climactic day of the Feast, Jesus took his stand. He cried out, "If anyone thirsts, let him come to me and drink. Rivers of living water will brim and spill out of the depths of anyone who believes in me this way, just as the Scripture says."
>
> —JOHN 7:37–38 MSG

The Feast of Tabernacles referred to in the above text was one of three major pilgrimage feasts for Jewish people, along with Passover and the Festival of Weeks. It took place at the end of September through the beginning of October in our calendar and was a joyful festival like our harvest Thanksgiving, a time to remember God's provision for his people when they wandered in the wilderness for forty years. During this time, each family constructed a temporary shelter of branches to last for the seven days of the feast. (I have to say, my son would have loved that!) Pilgrims gathered from every part of Palestine to celebrate with their families, building their shelters on the streets and on rooftops. It must have been quite a sight! Unlike Passover, which contained the solemn reminder of how they had been spared on that night of bloodshed in Egypt by the sprinkling of lamb's blood, the Feast of Tabernacles was a party!

Everyone in Judea might have been ready to celebrate, but the clock was ticking down for Jesus. It's one thing to turn water into wine at a wedding (the religious leaders could almost put that down to a party trick). But when Jesus healed a man who was paralyzed, he crossed a line. Not only had he healed a man who had been paralyzed for thirty-eight years, he did it on the Sabbath. Then he told the man to roll up his mat and walk. When the Jewish leaders asked the man why he was breaking the law by carrying a bedroll on the Sabbath, he told them, "The man who made me well told me to. He said, 'Take your bedroll and start walking'" (John 5:11 MSG). They asked who told him to do it but the man didn't know who Jesus was, and Jesus had slipped away into the crowd after he had healed him. I imagine that he was told if he ever saw the man again to find out who he was and report back to them.

A little while later Jesus saw the man in the temple court and told him that he looked wonderful. They talked for long enough for the man to work out that this man was Jesus of Nazareth, so he told the religious leaders he had seen the man again and his name was Jesus. So they went after Jesus for breaking the law. Ignoring the miracle of a man who had been unable to walk for almost forty years, they honed in on the fact that Jesus "worked" on the Sabbath. John records in his Gospel, "But Jesus defended himself. 'My Father is working straight through, even on the Sabbath. So am I.' That really set them off. The Jews were now not only out to expose him; they were out to kill him" (5:17–18 MSG).

Everywhere Jesus turned there was either open hatred, lack of understanding, or even biting sarcasm from the lips of his own brothers. It's a terrible thing to be ridiculed by those you love. Perhaps you have been there. It is a piercing wound. As the Feast of Tabernacles approached Jesus remained in Galilee, purposely staying away from Judea, knowing that his enemies were waiting for him, looking for the right moment to have him killed. His brothers said to him, "Why don't you leave here and go up to the Feast so your disciples can get a good look at the works you do? No one who intends to be publicly known does everything behind the scenes. If you're serious about what you are doing, come out in the open and show the world" (John 7:3–4 MSG). John went on to write that his brothers didn't believe in him. Jesus simply told them that it wasn't the right time, so his brothers left and went to Jerusalem together. But Jesus did go—he went in secret.

The Jewish authorities were watching for him—in fact, the whole crowd was buzzing about this man. Some said that he was a good man, but others thought he deceived people. Halfway through the feast, Jesus began to publicly teach in the temple courtyard. There was dissention in the crowd about Jesus, and there had been since the feeding of the five thousand, which had caused a lot of people who called themselves his disciples to stop following him. Jesus was stirring things up, which made people nervous. Not just nervous, but confused. During Jesus' teaching the people were amazed that he knew so much but wasn't one of their rabbis. Then Jesus asked the question of the religious leaders in front of the crowd, "Why are you trying to kill me?" I imagine that the conversation in the booths that night revolved around what they had seen and heard that day. According to John 7:25–27, they had much to talk about.

"This is the person they've been looking for!"

"But if he's a bad man, why didn't they arrest him?"

"Perhaps the Scribes and Pharisees know that he is the Messiah."

"But we know where this man is from. When Messiah comes, he will just appear as if from nowhere."

Mixed in with faith was superstition. Some still held to the belief that Messiah would miraculously appear, perhaps on the pinnacle of the temple. But after hearing Jesus teach, there were many in the crowd who were swayed to believe, which simply fueled the determination of the religious leaders to kill Jesus before he caused any more trouble. Remaining on God's timetable, no matter the atmosphere of the moment, Jesus chose the last and most holy day of the feast to make this declaration, "If anyone thirsts, let him come to me and drink. Rivers of living water will brim and spill out of the depths of anyone who believes in me this way, just as the Scripture says" (John 7:37 MSG). The feast itself lasted for seven days, followed by an eighth day of personal consecration and a sacrifice. What Jesus did was shocking. He took everything that was familiar to them and declared himself to be the fulfillment of it.

Each day during the feast, there would be a procession of priests out to the Pool of Siloam where they would draw water to take back to the temple and pour out on the altar. On this final, most holy day, Jesus stood up and in a loud voice said, "If you are thirsty, come to me!" Jesus was changing all the rules. God had provided water to his people in the wilderness but it had never been enough to satisfy them. Now Jesus was saying, "Believe!" It would not be enough any more to follow all the rituals and rules. A personal step of faith was required but the reward was over-the-top. To every man, woman, and child who believed in Christ, rivers of living water would overflow from them and touch everything and everyone around them.

What Jesus was promising was what every wanderer in every desert, spiritual or physical, has ever longed for. Ezekiel wrote about this promise: "I'll give you a new heart, put a new spirit in you. I'll remove the stone heart from your body and replace it with a heart that's God-willed, not self-willed" (36:26 MSG). That promise stands today for you. If you are finding yourself in a dry place in your life, Jesus stands up and, in a voice loud enough to cut through the other voices in your head, says, "If you are thirsty, come to me and drink. If you believe in me, rivers of water—not just water but living water—will flow deep inside and bubble up until they are over the top." What a promise!

31

In Your Own Words

PATSY CLAIRMONT

When I was a little girl my parents gave me a green metal Tom Thumb Typewriter for Christmas. I was beyond joy. You know that euphoric feeling where you want to go door-to-door to tell the world of your good fortune? Like the Avon lady. I've never been one to hold in a happy secret. I have way too much helium in me for that. Besides I'm the type of person you just have to look at to know I'm chomping at the bit to make an "announcement." And this super-duper type-writing machine seemed worthy of a proclamation. For me this gift was over-the-top!

> *The pen is mightier than the sword, but a well-aimed typewriter packs good punch too.*
>
> —ANON

Because of its tinny design every time I struck a letter, you could hear it reverberate off the paper all the way to Nebraska. I didn't mind the ricocheting clang, because I felt so grown up finger-picking my way over the keyboard. But sometimes the ink-soaked ribbon would droop, and I would try to straighten it out only to get black ink all over my hands, the machine, and the papers. I didn't mind that either, in fact, it made me feel quite professional. Now as for my mom, she wasn't as fond of the Picasso ink blotches smeared across my clothes. (Well, I had to wipe my hands off somewhere.)

Even as a youngster I loved anything to do with words and their formation, so I didn't mind the awkward traits of this child's machine. It seemed a small price to pay to be able to pretend I had great things to say. I often typed up playful ditties hopeful that one day I'd be discovered. Here's one from long ago and far away: "Up in the clouds and the sky so high the angels play in the soft moving sky, With their harps of gold and silver too they'll never wear out in the clouds of blue."

Well, we all have to start somewhere. Unfortunately my writing career was put on hold when the ink in the ribbon dried, some of the keys began to stick, and after being dropped a few times, the typewriter was finally silenced.

Then my mom bought a used grown-up typewriter for herself. A hefty Remington. It had no letters identifying the keys so that one could learn how to type without peeking. It weighed about the same as their Oldsmobile, and I remembered thinking it was really tall, but I'm sure that was because I really wasn't. Mom had the typewriter sitting out on her desk and I thought it quite handsome and official. It looked to be full of mystery that was just waiting to be coaxed out.

I developed a love/hate relationship with that bull-dozer of a machine as I tried to perfect my typing skills, which I never did. Even after taking typing in high school I had to hunt and peck. And now after decades, not to mention many books later, I am still like a chicken tapping away at the earth trying to find a solitary seed. Yet I still love to watch words appear on my computer screen and crowd together in a friendly manner.

I realize it is not my love of machines, even as fancy as our laptops have become, that keeps me bent over a keyboard searching for the right combination of letters to express my thoughts. But instead it is that love for words and their ability to sing and cry, yell and whisper, dance and recline, love and regret, yodel and hum that keeps me propped in front of a screen watching to see what happens next.

*I love writing. I love the swirl and swing of words as
they tangle with human emotions.*

—James Michener

I'm told if we write with the opposite hand instead of
the preferred one we will tap into all kinds of new
thoughts and old emotions. I tried it and realized why I
like keyboards . . . it's readable. But I must confess I did
touch some spongy emotions when I asked and answered
some personal questions. Now whether that was the
power of suggestion or a legitimate way to trace emotional
wiring I'm not sure, but it could be worth your effort.

I once typed a piece about my favorite doll from my
childhood and learned that much can be slipped under a
bib and tucked inside of booties and those feelings have a
long shelf life. Who knew? I'm convinced now that I must
have whispered little girl secrets to my doll because they
came out of hiding as I wrote about her.

Yes, I'm persuaded that writing, when it tangles with
emotions, can bring forth insights, understanding, and
growth. I know my life is wider and deeper because of the
willingness of writers who would dare to hold their lives
to the light and let me take a look.

I tend to be a bit of a romantic at heart and appreciate
a somewhat frilly writer. As a young adult I enjoyed Lucy

Maud Mongomery (1872-1942) the author of the Anne of Green Gables series and Emily of New Moon. I am amazed that out of the heart of a woman who suffered such hardship came such beauty, humor, and triumph.

Years ago I visited Prince Edwards Island where Lucy grew up. At the time of my visit I was told that flights from Japan were booked a full year in advance with families coming to see the birthplace of this writer. Lucy could not have imagined that her work would live on far beyond the days, where in the midst of her sadness she penned joy.

I love the work of Charles Spurgeon (1834-1892). His heart spills into his sermons and devotionals. I can sit and soak in a single line for days and still not empty all its contents. It's not just his poetic style that captures me but most certainly the truth he trumpets within it.

Spurgeon suffered from clinical depression and found himself often given to bouts of tears for no apparent reason. And yet in spite of his medical melancholy Charles wrote countless books and was believed to have preached almost thirty-six thousand sermons impacting millions. And that was before the days of televisions and Internet broadcasts.

Charles Haddon Spurgeon died young, he was fifty-seven years old, and yet the impact of what he wrote so eloquently starting at nineteen years old, lives on today and I'm sure, if the Lord tarries, will continue into future generations.

A current writer who fills my cup is Charles R. Swindoll. Yes, he's my friend Luci's brother, but I was reading Chuck's work long before I met Luci. And today Chuck is also my winter pastor. My husband and I stay in Texas for four months taking shelter from Michigan's bitter bite. While there we rush to hear Chuck, and I usually am weepy for the first month of Sundays for the sheer privilege of hearing such beautiful and powerful preaching.

Chuck's writing is sparkling clear and deeply penetrating. I love his humor and his ability to turn a phrase into a spigot of fresh water. He is a lifetime student of God's Word and a voracious, expansive reader. Chuck is not casual regarding his calling but pursues it with passion and excellence.

And no, in case you're wondering, Chuck's not depressed since that seems to be a theme with my other favorite writers. Actually I've never noted a gloomy spell to overtake Chuck. He exhibits, even in his hard seasons, an underlying, if not overflowing joy. Chuck has published over seventy books.

Early on in my reading career, I devoured *Strike the Original Match*, Chuck's study on marriage. I was impacted by his inspiring *Second Wind: A Fresh Run at Life*, which I have read repeatedly throughout the years. Many of his titles like *The Finishing Touch*, remain on my all-time-favorites list. His words seem timeless making rereading a worthwhile pursuit.

I do love words, whether typed, penned, printed, or engraved, if they marry well on a page and invite me on the honeymoon I'm packing my bags to tag along. Hopefully we go somewhere fun. Words when they bump up against each other in a friendly manner can make us laugh out loud, like the magnet on my refrigerator . . .

"Only one shopping day until tomorrow."

Well, I thought it was funny. My husband, not so much. But what about the one that says . . .

"I'll always love you Mom, but I'll never forgive you for washing my face with spit on your hankie."

Now that's a grinner if ever there was one. Try this quote on for size . . .

"Youth is wholly experimental."

Thank you Robert Louis Stevenson I needed that chuckle.

See what I mean? Words can entertain us, educate us, and inspire us. I love Violeta Parra's poetic perspective . . .

"Don't cry when the sun is gone the tears won't let you see the stars."

Guess what? I just Googled Tom Thumb Typewriter,

and there are still some floating around from the 1950's. One lady was asking fifty dollars for a just slightly less than functional one. (Boy, could I identify.) You know, it would almost be worth the visual memories to have it around . . . almost. I'll sleep on it. While I ponder that purchase, remember: words can be an endless stream of artistry . . . that can take you over the top. So get out your version of a Tom Thumb and write, girlfriends, write!

32

Crooked Places

MARILYN MEBERG

've been thinking about the word *crooked*. The Bible uses the word often. It seems to indicate that crooked places are not a good thing. Isaiah 40 says for God's people to "make a highway for the LORD through the wilderness. Make a straight, smooth road through the desert for our God.... Straighten out the curves and smooth off the rough spots" (vv. 3–4 NLT). Proverbs 11:3 states, "The integrity of the upright guides them, but the crookedness of the treacherous destroys them" (NRSV). The theme is continued in Philippians 2:15 as Paul declares that the children of God are "in the midst of a crooked and perverse generation" (NKJV). These kinds of biblical statements inspire believers to pray that God would intervene in our lives and make the crooked places straight. We assume crooked places are to be avoided.

I recently have learned a new thing about rough and crooked places: what can appear to be a crooked place can actually be a place where God goes before me, straightening out the curves and smoothing the rough spots. I recently experienced what looked to me like a rough place that totally threatened my security. But I was only seeing the crookedness, while God was getting me ready to see his straightening.

Luci Swindoll, Mary Graham, Lisa Whelchel, and I were flying together to Rwanda in February 2009 for a World Vision-sponsored opportunity, to see what they are doing for orphaned and needy children in that impoverished country. We had successfully completed our flights from Dallas to London and taxied in to the airport in Nairobi, Kenya, shortly before midnight. Because we did not want to overnight in Kenya, we voted to dash for the last flight of the night to Kigali, Rwanda. That meant going through customs in Nairobi, claiming our bags, and reticketing them to Rwanda.

All was going well until we ran into an issue with the girl in Kenyan customs. "Where is your visa?" she asked.

"Well, we don't have one because we aren't staying in Kenya," we replied.

"Where is your visa?"

"Well you see, we were told we did not need one. We

are catching the Kenya Air flight to Rwanda which leaves in thirty minutes . . . so we are a little pressed for time."

"You need a visa."

Sighing deeply, we asked where we needed to go to get a visa.

Of course, while we stood in the visa line, our flight to Rwanda took off. Now we truly did need a visa; we were going to spend the night in Nairobi. Not only did we need a visa, we needed to rebook our flights to Rwanda, and, looking nervously around the Nairobi airport, maybe a room for the night.

After managing to get our visas, we delegated our duties: Mary would rebook tickets to Rwanda; Lisa would keep an eye on Luci, who's prone to wander in search of adventure; and I would see if our bags were still in baggage claim. Being a woman of faith, I could not imagine someone hoping to find treasure from unclaimed American luggage had not stolen the bags. I mentally calculated how I could stand to wear the clothes I was in for the next ten days; at least my clothes started out clean. I could smell the lingering sweet scent of fabric softener from Lisa's sweatshirt. I figured she should be good for a few more days. When I arrived at the baggage claim area, I was not allowed to enter. The one young man "back there" did not speak English and seemed bored with my gestures depicting desperation and need. I figured our bags probably weren't there anyway.

Then it occurred to me the people at British Air might be able to help figure out the bag scene. They were extremely courteous, but dubious about the safety and location of our bags. Three young British Air agents (Kenyans) conferred together behind their hands—they need not have hidden their voices, because I had no idea what they were saying or in what language they might be saying it. Then one of the young men said, with a decided accent but sweet smile, "I will get your bags." I followed him to baggage claim. The bags were there; they had not been stolen. I applied to once again become a woman of faith.

With our bags in tow, we made our way to a section of seats within shouting distance of Mary who was still in line to rebook our flights. With triumph, I hollered over to her, "Hey! Our bags!" Within minutes a young Kenyan man walked toward me. He looked pleasant, was wearing a British Air shirt, but was eyeballing me quizzically. He asked where I was going. I told him three other women and I were going to Rwanda but we had missed that flight and were rebooking to leave in the morning. He stared at me briefly and then asked. "Why . . . why are you going to Rwanda?"

I said we were on a World Vision trip. As I was about to explain the trip more fully, he leapt toward me. "World Vision? Did you say World Vision?" His eyes grew big as saucers, and he fairly shouted, "World Vision saved my life! My sister, two brothers, and I were orphaned. Our parents died of AIDS. We had nowhere to live except the streets. I was so afraid my little sister would be forced into prostitution. Then World Vision found us and saved all of us." With huge tears in his eyes he said over and over, "You . . . you . . . World Vision saved my family!"

Then our new friend, named Peter, leaned over to me and said, "You are probably not safe here, but I will take care of you, just like World Vision took care of me."

True to his word, Peter never left us throughout the booking of new flights, finding a hotel, and managing transportation to that hotel. It was nearly 3:00 a.m. when we stood at the hotel counter. We were grateful but only for a moment—a room was not an option because none of us had Kenyan currency. We tried to put the rooms on our credit cards, but our cards were denied. The companies were suspicious of attempted use of an American Express card at 3:00 a.m. from Nairobi.

Peter stepped over to the desk and said, "You have to give my friends a room!" The clerk said he had to be paid or it was impossible. Gathering into a huddle, Peter told us we could get a room if we paid for it in American currency. We looked at each other helplessly. We had purposely brought very little cash with the intention of using a card if need be. We were basically broke. Nevertheless we emptied our purses in a combined effort to find money, possibly hidden in purse corners. Maybe it was because we were tired, but we all got giggly as we shouted out the contents of our purses. "Hey, I found a ten . . . here's a twenty . . . found another twenty! OK, we need fifty more!" We found enough, and we were in our rooms by 3:30 a.m.

After a short but grateful rest, we were taken back to the Nairobi airport. On the way we talked about our extraordinary encounter with Peter, how creative it was of God to provide that meeting, how helpful Peter had been and his determination to not leave us until we were safely in our hotel rooms. We had all hugged him good-bye the night before and told him we'd tell everyone at World Vision about him. To our amazement, when we pulled up to the curb at the airport, there was Peter waiting for us. It was his day off, but he said he could not sleep in; he had to know for sure we got safely on board our flight to Rwanda. Wearing his British Air tags, he escorted us to our gate with no waiting in any lines.

We held a hasty conference to see if anyone had money left in her purse; we wanted to give it to Peter as a love gift. We managed to pool twenty-five dollars. Mary reached out for Peter's hand in an effort to give it to him. Drawing back in horror, he said, "No-oh-no! World Vision saved my life. They gave me an education and provided food. We had so many needs. I am so happy to help you with your needs."

So there, standing in front of our gate and obstructing passenger traffic, we wrapped our arms around each other and prayed. Tearfully we thanked God for what he had done and will continue to do in Peter's life. We thanked God for how he had used Peter in ours. On the short flight to Kigali, capital city of Rwanda, I pondered how creatively God had made a "straight, smooth road" for all of us. In my unimaginative thinking, a smooth road would have meant no missed flight in Nairobi and an on-time arrival in Rwanda. But look what I would have missed if God had only done the expected, hoped for, and planned on! I repeatedly learn that God is never boring: he is always over-the-top. His ways are not my ways, and as he works in his way, I am enriched and totally in awe.

33

Last-Minute Trip

NICOLE C. MULLEN

Not too long ago I received a last-minute request to go to Sweden to sing. I weighed the options, prayed about it, and felt no adverse check on the inside, so I agreed to do it. According to the calendar, we would have a bus date in Michigan on Thursday night, and after that concert we would leave by midnight Eastern time, drive home overnight to Nashville, get off the bus, and take a plane to Europe. I knew it was a possible formula for crankiness, due to a lack of sleep (and other areas I'm working on conquering), so from the start, my thoughts were to upgrade whatever tickets the promoter had purchased if they had not bought first-class tickets from the get-go. Then I would have a better chance of getting rest and helping my flesh to act like a Christian.

When it came time to purchase the tickets, I was notified that we, and not the promoter, were in charge of paying for the flights. *Hmm . . . OK, OK, no big deal . . . honest mistake*, I thought. After a brief search, we miraculously found tickets that matched our desired time frame and stayed within the amount we wanted to spend. There was one catch though—they were not upgradeable. Because we were running out of time, we decided to go ahead and purchase them, and we were rapidly approaching the window of time when the price of the tickets would go up tremendously. We would see what could be done about the upgrades later.

Finally the date on the calendar arrived, and so far things were playing out the way I had imagined. The concert in Michigan was great. We had lots of fun; we danced hard, sang loud, told stories, hugged necks, and signed CDs and pictures until we were literally in violation of exceeding the building's curfew. (Side note: My favorite part of the night is not necessarily being on the stage, though I enjoy it immensely. What I really love is being able to see and touch the people afterwards. And I always feel that if the people can hang around for hours after a concert, then so can I—unless I have a plane to catch or the timer on my right eye has expired, and now I'm so tired that I'm looking cross-eyed in everyone's pictures.) So this night we stayed in the foyer, signing until the end, even with the eye thing and the plane to catch the next day. When it was over, we said good-bye, and we were on the road again. The bus drove by night and I prayed that I would sleep well. Still, I was really looking forward to the window seat that my road manager, Lisa, had secured for me on the two flights we were to take to Sweden. I thought, OK, *if tomorrow's upgrade doesn't happen, the window is the next best thing. I'll snuggle up against it, and let the rhythm of the engines put me to sleep.* I had a plan, and in theory, it should have worked.

As soon as the tour bus pulled into town, I began preparing for my trip to the airport. Once there, the airline attendant who checked my bags was very kind, and even looked into upgrading my ticket. My hopes were up for a moment, and he seemed to share my disappointment when he learned that there was nothing that could be done. I told myself, OK, *no biggie. I still have my all-time favorite flying position—the window seat—plus this first flight is only about an hour.* So we went up into the air and then back down again, and I was content. In this I was going to give thanks. During this trip, I was in the process of reading and listening to two books. One was about eighteen hours long—an audio book called *Inside the Revolution* by Joel C. Rosenberg. (I highly recommend it.) The other was an actual paper copy of *Jesus Freaks: Revolutionaries* (stellar as well). Through these books I heard the Lord challenging me to "come up" and not to be lured by the comforts around me. I heard in my spirit, and in my mind, that the call of God is not about what I find convenient. Taking up a cross, daily, is not meant to be convenient.

Once the first flight was over, and before we hopped on the plane to fly overseas, I remembered sharing these thoughts with Lisa. It was becoming clear to me that how we act and react to even the smallest things in life is what will prepare us for the greater things that God has for us, even if that greater thing requires suffering for his name. I needed to share this, to help me stay accountable, just in case. So before boarding the second plane, the flight attendant called several names, including ours, over to the desk. She told us to wait in line while she made some changes. From what I understood by the conversation she was currently having, the people in front of us were upgraded, in order to let a family sit together. My hopes began to soar.

So after waiting for about a ten-minute span, it was our turn. The flight attendant told us that the airline had changed aircrafts, and our seats were being changed as well—but not to business or first class. We were being booted from our window seats to an aisle and middle seat.

On an international flight. That meant *no* window to lie against, no seven hours of rest. I started thinking, *How am I going to keep from looking like a bobblehead when I sleep?* Lisa was seated in the middle seat between a man we did not know and me. Since she is on the skinny side of life, her shoulder would be of no comfort to me in the event of a head slip. I recognized this as a small test on the subject of being a "comfort Christian." So I immediately decided to guard my mouth and attitude with the Lord's help, and give thanks for these less-than-stellar circumstances.

Soon, what could have been annoying became quite humorous. Throughout the night our male row-mate, began to snore—very loudly. It became impossible to tune him out, or to fall asleep. I tossed and turned in the aisle seat, praying that by the morning I would have built a little more character. Somewhere in the wee hours of the night, I got really giddy. I found myself tickled at the scenario and people around us "mean-mugging" (that is, giving dirty looks) at this guy for keeping them awake, while he himself enjoyed la-la land, never noticing the ruckus he was causing.

Again, even in the small things I was then, and I am now, challenged to *do* the scriptures and not just recite them. We are commanded in 1 Thessalonians 5:18: "In everything give thanks, for this is God's will for you in

Christ Jesus" (NASB). After reexamining this verse, I am relieved to see that it does not say "for everything." The Lord is not commanding me to be thankful for the annoying or even devastatingly evil things that may happen in life, but he is commanding that, in the midst of all these things, his will for me, for us, is that we be thankful. One may ask, "If life is dealing you a bitter blow, then what is there to be thankful for?" My answer, though limited from its fullness due to my finite understanding and vocabulary, would be that even in our toughest times, God is at work and we are not alone. We are known by the one who created the heavens, the earth, the stars, and the planets, the seas, and all that live within and above them; and we are loved. Though I may not understand how this current pain or inconvenience will be used for my benefit, I can trust Christ when his words to me are: "In all things God works for the good of those who love him, who have been called according to his purpose" (Romans 8:28 NIV). He never promised that all things would be good, but that he would work them together for our good.

It is very much like the chocolate chip cookie analogy. Before we are able to bite into that warm, perfectly baked morsel of delight, we must consider that it did not start out that way. And though I love the end result of blended ingredients, I would not want to eat them all separately—except for the chocolate chips, of course. See, I would have to pass on the raw eggs, the scoops of flour. The taste of the baking soda that's needed for dough expansion would not resemble anything close to the cookie I desire, nor would a stick of butter. On the other hand, if all I used were the sweet ingredients, like the sugar and chocolate chips, I would be left with no cookie and one more cavity. But if I were to give all of these same ingredients to a baker who had won all kinds of awards, titles, and accolades, he would be able to take the bitter, the salty, the sweet, the buttery, the bland, the smallness of the chips, and work it together into something wonderfully tasty, far beyond what the average cook could produce.

The same is true in our daily lives. God has promised to take the bland and sometimes common things of life, the sweet morsels, the big and small things, the dangerous and hard-to-swallow events, and work them all together for the good of those who love him. Imagine the possibilities!

34

Get Off Your Rocker

◖ LUCI SWINDOLL

Hollywood's New Darling" was the newspaper headline that first caught my eye. Then it was the picture of ninety-seven-year-old Mae Laborde, who's been an actor for the last six years. In March 2007 there was quite a stir about this "up and coming" movie star. At the age of ninety-three, Mae decided she wanted to be in films. "I'm just a natural," she said with a sweet-as-peaches-and-cream smile when talking with folks who were curious about her success. At four feet ten inches, with snow-white hair and rosy-red cheeks, the woman appears to be the hottest ticket in town.

Mae's acting career was actually launched by columnist Steve Lopez (her former neighbor), in a 2002 *Los Angeles Times* story when he wrote about this little old lady barreling up and down the neighborhood streets of Santa Monica in one of those gigantic 1977 Oldsmobile Delta 88s. She was so small and the car so big that Steve said she looked like a "cricket driving a tank." That description appealed to talent agent Sherrie Spillane (former wife of Mickey Spillane) who insisted on meeting this little bundle of dynamite. The two of them got together for a tea-leaf reading (Ms. Laborde's hobby), and the next thing Sherrie knew, she had a new client. Golly! Mae's been in an HBO special—*Real Time with Bill Maher*—as well as a cheerleader on ESPN. In addition, she's appeared in an episode of *Mad TV* and was in a couple commercials—one for Lexus and another for JP Morgan Chase Bank. The woman gets around.

Every now and then somebody asks her secret to living a long life. Without hesitation, she tells them, "Don't ever retire." This onetime department store clerk and bookkeeper adds that older people who are contemplating stepping aside from real life should "get off your rocker and get out there to see what's going on." The most recent thing I've read about her is that she landed a small role in a Ben Stiller movie. Ms. Laborde will never be old, even if she lives to be one hundred and fifty. Go Mae!

What is it about some people that make them retain their resilient spirit no matter their age? Where is the fountain of youth from which they drink? Don't we all want to find it . . . and swallow great gulps of it until the day the Lord takes us home? I certainly do! I want to meet the people who believe, along with Isaiah, "I will be your God through all your lifetime, yes, even when your hair is white with age"(46:4 TLB).

It's rare to find individuals who even *want* to live into their nineties, much less take on Hollywood at that age. But Mae Laborde was the exception to all rules it seems. At eighty-nine, she took a police training course just for fun; she still cooks her own meals, paints, raises tomatoes in her garden, and sells them to a local restaurant. Ms. Laborde is one of those delightful wind-up toys that never stops entertaining the rest of us with her incomparable energy and *joie de vivre*. I hope I'm just like her when I grow up.

Actually, Mae's got me beat by twenty years, but I have several friends about her age, and I've observed them very carefully as I've taken mental notes on how they face life. I can think of three women right now who are a testimony to aging well. They remind me of those last few verses in Psalm 92:12–13 that read: "Good people will prosper like palm trees, grow tall like Lebanon cedars; transplanted to GOD's courtyard, they'll grow tall in the presence of God, lithe and green, virile still in old age" (MSG).

There's Rebecca, my eighty-seven-year-old friend who's blind in one eye and walks with a cane. Her daughter and I are friends and have been for many years. It was through her that I met and fell in love with her mother. She has an indomitable spirit and an encyclopedic memory. Reading is her favorite pastime, but as her sight has decreased, it's become harder to make out the words. So Rebecca uses a magnifying glass. One day she and I were talking, and I asked her to name a book she had always wanted to read but had never gotten around to it. Immediately, she said, "Oh Luci, I'd like to read *The Gulag Archipelago* by Solzhenitsyn. I've heard it is so interesting. I know it's a big book, so I'd probably have to figure out a way to hold it, but I could do that." Before the day was over, I bought her a paperback copy, gift-wrapped it, and took it to her. She was thrilled to death. Without hesitation, she tore it in half, took out her magnifying glass and began reading the first half. Within two weeks, she had read the whole thing and given me an amazing book report.

When we're together, we talk about words and their origins, poetry, what's going on in the world, and how times have changed since she was a youngster. Not a day goes by that Rebecca doesn't read the newspaper, check the stock market, and catch up on her favorite funnies. She's a wonder and I hope I'm just like her when I grow up.

Alberta's ninety-nine and going strong—she's another friend I so deeply admire. I was with her not long ago in Shreveport, where she lives in an assisted living facility. I was so impressed with the place, and most especially with Alberta's little suite. It was spotlessly clean, well-arranged, full of pictures and keepsakes, with a view out the window of blooming azaleas. Alberta has four children, all of whom adore her and visit her all the time. Prior to entering this facility, she had a stationary bike, and through the years had ridden a total of 70,000 miles in her exercise program.

I asked Alberta if she got very much mail. "No," she said. "But that's okay. I know almost everyone in the building, and we've become friends." She has a great attitude about life and her circumstances . . . and a terrific sense of humor. I asked if it would be all right if I wrote her every now and then. She was pleased and seemed honored that I wanted to. Her daughter gave me her address that day, and so far I've written about twenty postcards from different cities when I'm traveling with Women of Faith, bringing her up to date on our conferences. Or, if I have a weekend off, I often write just to chat and tell her I'm thinking of her.

Alberta could bemoan her fate to be in an assisted living facility, or she could be down in the mouth about the food or accommodations or the fact that her age prevents her from doing all she wants to do . . . but she's not. She has chosen to have a wonderful, uplifting attitude about life and the situation in which she finds herself. I want to be just like Alberta when I grow up.

And finally, there's Evelyn. She lives alone in a little bitty house near a college campus. Unafraid and in her nineties, she doesn't need a companion to stay with her because, "I have Jesus," she says. Evelyn sings and quotes scripture to her family and acquaintances and has a far-reaching prayer ministry, covering friends all over the world. When I see her, she encourages me by simply being herself. When college students come over to bring cookies or a hot meal, Evelyn makes tea, and they sit together and tell stories, reminiscing about her fascinating life. Evelyn isn't afraid of money problems or impending sickness or being by herself or what anybody might think of her . . . because, "I have Jesus." It's as though she lives a heavenly life already because she's not scared of anything. Very relaxed and happy, Christ has made her complete in himself. I hope to be Evelyn when I grow up!

These four wonderful women show me over and over what it is to be strong in old age. They got off their rockers to see what was going on and liked what they saw. Each one has determined to live fully in spite of all that comes with aging. We can do that, too, my friends. Here's what it takes: Pursue your dream. Use your mind. Choose your attitude and lose your fear. When we decide to live that way, we'll never grow old. The apostle James captured it very well when he wrote in chapter 1, verse 12, "Anyone who meets a testing challenge head-on and manages to stick it out is mighty fortunate. . . . the reward is life and more life" (MSG).

I raise my glass to you—Mae, Rebecca, Alberta, and Evelyn! If I had a big old 1977 Oldsmobile Delta 88, I'd come get you all, and we'd barrel up and down the neighborhood streets together, painting the town red. And Mae . . . I'd let you drive.

35

Living a Life of Joy

MARY GRAHAM

L ife is difficult. Jesus said in the sixteenth chapter of John, "In this world, you will have trouble" (v. 33 NIV). I'm not sure if we should take it as a promise, or a severe warning. On any given day, of any given year, in cities and villages all over the world, with families of all sizes, rich and poor, life can be difficult. We all know it and have experienced it. Some days and years feel hopeless; others just feel challenging. Few people I know, have met, or even read about are trouble-free.

And yet, trouble seems to take me by surprise. When we meet face-to-face, I find myself thinking, *How did you get in here? I wasn't expecting Trouble!* It's impossible to avoid so we learn to manage it, to live with it, pray it through, and hold on for dear life. Most of us will do whatever it takes to survive the challenges of this life. That's why I want to, as Luci Swindoll says so often, "learn to live the life out of every day." We can't avoid life's pain but when we can, we can make the most of what we have. We can enjoy our friends, family, the work God has given us to accomplish, and savor the moments he gives us.

The truth of this came home to me about twelve years ago when I still lived in Orlando. I had a wonderful friend who lived there, Ann Wright. She was very dear to me. She and her husband, both at least ten years my senior, had been married fifty years and had two grown children. I loved that couple. We often worked and traveled together in our ministry with Campus Crusade for Christ, and every day with them was a delight. After Christmas one year, I got a call from Ann, who wanted to ask me a favor. She hemmed and hawed and was very hesitant to make her request known. Finally I had to drag it out of her. She said she'd actually been wanting to ask me something for several weeks but could not muster her courage. Her husband, Sid, had the sad misfortune of being born on New Year's Eve. As a result, he'd never had a birthday party in his life. (Who goes to a birthday party on New Year's Eve?) Knowing I've always had a knack for hosting live events, she wondered if I could give him a party for his seventieth birthday. In two days. On New Year's Eve. And she wanted it to be a surprise.

I had no doubt we could do it and it would be tons of fun. Fortunately, Luci Swindoll was visiting me over the holidays, so I had that great resource to bring to bear as we planned the world's best birthday party ever. First we hurriedly made a guest list of about thirty people and phoned everyone. They couldn't wait to come. Even if they had plans, they planned to change them. So we had people, and Ann was going to prepare the food and buy the birthday cake. All we needed was entertainment. So . . .

Luci and I decided we'd create a little variety show working only with what we had. It was long before the TV show *America's Got Talent*, but looking back on it, I think it might have been our original idea and someone stole it from us. We called everyone we knew coming to the party and asked them if they had any kind of gift or unique skill that would qualify them to be on the "stage." Before long we had a party going with a very colorful lineup of great stars to entertain us. And what a lineup! Tina told us the only thing she could do was tap dance and she'd not done it since she was a child. She did mention she'd been quite good at it so we couldn't wait to see it. She was wonderful—but the only wooden stage we could find that was suitable was a three-by-three-foot breadboard. She needed music, which was fine because Judy could play "Anchors Aweigh" on her trumpet (which she'd also not played in several years).

Once all of that came together, we were beside ourselves with how great this party could be. What we lacked in true talent, we were making up for in sheer enthusiasm. By the night before the party, we had Ney doing a very funny skit from camp from the 1950s; Luci sang a song from a penny opera called "Egyptian Ella." The list went on and on. I, of course, was the emcee. I have to say, I gave grand introductions for such spectacular talent. The only small thing about that party was the budget. I'm not sure anyone spent a dime except the one who bought the cake (which, incidentally, caught on fire when we lit the candles).

It was one of the most delightful evenings of our lives. At 2:00 a.m. we left the house, and there was a gorgeous full moon. Spontaneously, we all started singing at the top of our lungs, in three-part harmony, "See that moon shining way up high, like a diamond in the sky. He wants to go to bed, too, but he has to stay up and light the way for you . . ." How did we even know that song?

For years, people talked about that party, and those who'd been out of town never got over their disappointment of missing it. "Why didn't you tell us you were going to have such a fabulous party?" so many would say. And our answer was always the same, "Because we had no idea." The joy that filled the room that night cannot be measured and will never be forgotten. Within a year or two, the honoree, Sid, was diagnosed with cancer and spent several weeks in Houston at MD Anderson Clinic. Shortly after he was released, Ann, our dear most wonderful friend, was diagnosed with cancer as well and died a few months later. I will never recover from losing Ann. I loved her like a sister. And I will never regret being a part of what she always said was one of the best nights of her life.

It's so easy to feel as if we're running on empty. Our resources are limited and there is no more to give. We have no more time, energy, or money. So we struggle, worry, and fret. What if we didn't? What if we made the most of what we have? And more often than not, one person can turn the tide. I heard a true story of a family who went through a very sparse and difficult time. At one point the mother went to the kitchen and found nothing in the cupboard but a box of Bisquick and a box of Jell-O. As she was preparing those for dinner, she decided to make it a festive occasion in spite of the sparse menu. She set the table beautifully, used candlelight, fine china, and linens, played music, thought of clever questions for conversation, and served biscuits and Jell-O. In the end, the family enjoyed a fabulous evening. So much so that for years the children would ask, "Mama, when can we have biscuits and Jell-O for dinner again?"

So often it's not the tangible ingredients that make something special—it's the spirit, the tone that's set, the way something makes you feel, the connection people have with one another. That's what makes something unforgettable. We spend hours and months planning events at Women of Faith and Revolve. We want to be sure every minute is as it should be, that every message, drama, and bit of music is carefully chosen to make the weekends the best ever. But so often the memorable moments are those spontaneous times when we hear a story, meet someone new, have something completely unexpected happen that we'll never forget. We say to one another, "It's a God-thing." That's a strange-sounding phrase, but it captures how we feel. Real meaning more often than not supersedes the perfect or the planned. Joy is a gift God gives, not something we can engineer. When our hearts are open, we create a lot of room for possibility, and once we step into God's reality, our reality is no longer a limitation.

Life is hard, all but impossible at times. We can either spend our days and nights worrying about what's going on or what will happen next, or we can live fully and enjoy this life he's given us, even with its imperfections. Don't hold back. Never assume there's no time to celebrate, or at least don't assume this is not the time. Having a birthday on New Year's Eve? Not a problem. You've waited too long? It's never too late. Nothing to serve for dinner? Look in the cupboard. Life is difficult? Try living the life out of every day.

Notes

1. Used by permission from Nicole Johnson Newman.
2. Peggy Noonan, *On Speaking Well* (New York: Harper Collins, 1998), 162.
3. William Butler Yeats, *The Poems of W.B. Yeats* (Westport, CT: The Easton Press, 1976), 108.

TELL ME EVERYTHING

By Marilyn Meberg, available 3/30/2010

With the wisdom of a counselor and the whit of a comedian, Marilyn Meberg untangles the issues in women's lives that hold them back from a vibrant relationship with Christ.

FRIENDSHIP FOR GROWN-UPS

By Lisa Whelchel, available 5/4/2010

Former *Facts of Life* star Lisa Whelchel shares her experiences of growing up without true friends, how she learned to find and develop them as an adult through God's grace, and how readers should actively pursue meaningful friendships as adults.

DOING LIFE DIFFERENTLY

By Luci Swindoll, available 5/4/2010

An inspiring account of Luci Swindoll's courageous life that teaches readers how to live savoring each moment, how to let go of regrets, and how to embrace dreams.

THOMAS NELSON
Since 1798